Collaborating for Inquiry-Based Learning

Collaborating for Inquiry-Based Learning

School Librarians and Teachers Partner for Student Achievement

Virginia L. Wallace and
Whitney Norwood Husid

 LIBRARIES UNLIMITED

AN IMPRINT OF ABC-CLIO, LLC
Santa Barbara, California • Denver, Colorado • Oxford, England

Library of Congress Cataloging-in-Publication Data

Wallace, Virginia
  Collaborating for inquiry-based learning : school librarians and teachers partner for student achievement / Virginia L. Wallace and Whitney Norwood Husid.
    p. cm.
  Includes bibliographical references and index.
  ISBN 978-1-59884-850-2 (acid-free paper) — ISBN 978-1-59884-851-9 (ebook)
1. Inquiry-based learning. 2. Libraries and teachers—United States. 3. Libraries and education—United States. 4. School librarian participation in curriculum planning. I. Husid, Whitney Norwood. II. Title.
LB1027.23.W34   2011
371.3—dc23   2011018754

ISBN: 978-1-59884-850-2
EISBN: 978-1-59884-851-9

15 14 13 12 11   1 2 3 4 5

This book is also available on the World Wide Web as an eBook.
Visit www.abc-clio.com for details.

Libraries Unlimited
An Imprint of ABC-CLIO, LLC

ABC-CLIO, LLC
130 Cremona Drive, P.O. Box 1911
Santa Barbara, California 93116-1911

This book is printed on acid-free paper ∞

Manufactured in the United States of America

Copyright Acknowledgment

Excerpts and illustrations from Anderson & Krathwohl, *A Taxonomy for Learning, Teaching, and Assessing* are copyright (©) 2001, Addison Wesley Longman, Inc. Reproduced by permission of Pearson Education, Inc.

Contents

Chapter 1

Introduction

Change

There has been a paradigm shift. Silent school librarians shall perish. Historically, taking care of "things"—shelving books, placing orders, manning the circulation desk, conducting inventory, and maintaining a well-ordered space—occupied school librarians' days. Within these roles, school librarians sensed inviolate job security.

Today, there is a new focus: the students and their curricular as well as their literacy needs. School librarians educate, teach, collaborate, lead, and promote information and media literacies with the goal of preparing students for the twenty-first century. Otherwise, marginalization defines and diminishes school librarians as extracurricular and characterizes their position as support staff. Twenty-first-century librarians accept these expanded roles only when willing to change.

Change is uncomfortable, and library work represents a steady, linear, regular job—no frills with no alarms. Is that not how many librarians feel? Leave the change to other professions; school needs a routine, an eye toward completing the standards and giving the students some repetitious work in the school's comfort zone, the library media center (LMC). The LMC can represent a haven, a safe place not only for patrons and students, but also for many school librarians. However, school librarians must leave the library media center and take their expertise to teachers and students. When school librarians choose the comfort of the LMC over stepping into the curricular fray, they avoid the dynamics of the new roles for the new century. Moving outside the library media center allows partnering with classroom teachers to create a curriculum that elevates students beyond the core standards to a higher level of inquiry.

To deal with change, school librarians must manage multiple levels: internal, external, and systemic.

1. School librarians' perception of themselves as professionals changes when they accept the expanded definitions of their roles within the school environment.

2. Their publics' perception of their roles reflects a truer understanding of their value to both teaching and student learning.

3. Ultimately, the desired change impacts all building classrooms, teachers' attitudes, administrative outlook, student behaviors, and parental expectations, because the change is systemic.

Systemic change cannot occur in one area only. Systemic change requires fundamental changes in all areas of a system if it is to occur successfully in any one (Reigeluth & Garfinkle, 1994). School librarians' internal and external changes are requisite to affect the systemic change.

Barriers to Change

When school librarians accept the change agent role, the tendency to set up barriers, such as when, how, and why, will not immediately diminish. Most have a view of change that limits when to begin and how long to expect before the change occurs. When to begin and how to begin intertwine into "I cannot begin because it is too overwhelming!" Following that feeling is "Why begin? No one will listen. I'll face only resistance." Leaders tackle the when, how, and why. They look beyond the walls of their schools by utilizing their search expertise and by consulting experts and best practices. Vanguards and outliers extended their range of service long before the idea of the proactive school librarians as a teachers came into vogue. Hearing, reading, and seeing their successes on student achievement instill the challenge and give impetus to systemic change efforts. Deutschman (2005) separates myth from reality concerning change:

MYTH: Small, gradual changes are always easier to make and sustain.

REALITY: Radical, sweeping changes are often easier because they quickly yield benefits.

Benefits of Change

Such is the case for school librarians who usher in change. Better to sweep away how things have been done in favor of some quick starts on how they should be done. All talk about change begs the question, "Where?" Where is the change to take place? The answer is schoolwide, via collaborations between classroom teachers and school librarians. With collaboration, the students benefit in the areas of critical thinking, inquiry-based learning, research models, information seeking behaviors, standards, use of rubrics, authentic assessments, and reflection. As the American Association of School Librarians (AASL, 1998) has stated, "Student achievement is the bottom line."

Collaboration as a Change Agent

For classroom teachers and school librarians, the collaboration morphs over time to its highest level. Not achieving the apex in early attempts is not failure, but growth, development, and deeper, clearer comprehension. At first, both parties may have completely alien views of what they are doing in the partnership and where they are going. The common thread is students. Students hold the collaboration together while the instructional partners grope their way through the morass of yielding autonomy, sharing resources and ideas, accepting that "two heads are better than one," and building a bond that permeates the entire teaching/learning venue (see Figure 1.1).

These victories with collaboration garner administrative and parental support for what otherwise might be viewed as radically diminishing the state standards' focus. The administration's and parents' attention to state standards has arisen from fear of not meeting yearly

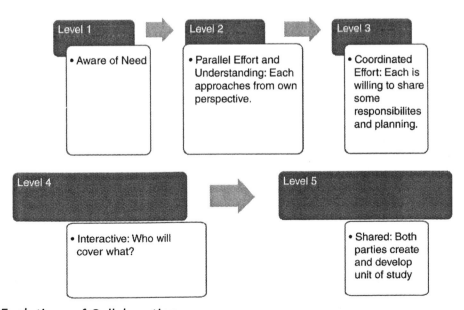

Figure 1.1 Evolutions of Collaboration.

progress or adequately preparing young people for college and good jobs. However, the improved pedagogy resulting from collaboration accelerates student achievement.

Who are the classroom teachers who will get on board early for these pedagogical changes? The kinds of classroom teachers who will step "out of the box": Passion Players, Innovators, Trailblazers, Pioneers, and Front Runners. They buy into the "Look It Up for a Report" versus "Inquiry Makes the Learning More Lasting" battle, where the ubiquitous report loses. These educational players willingly explore collaboration. They seek innovative approaches to teaching; they bring creativity and experimentation to the curriculum and want to improve their methods. They realize that collaboration affords everyone involved (classroom teachers, school librarians, and students) practice and learning with cutting-edge instructional strategies and processes.

Inquiry-Based Learning: Collaboration and Essential Questions

If education wishes to develop contemplative learners, how will the collaboration help? First must come an agreement between classroom teachers and school librarians that Bloom's Taxonomy represents a range of thinking skills from lower to higher order (Bloom, Eglehart, Furst, Hill, & Krathwohl, 1956). Second, they create assignments, projects, and activities that reinforce knowledge, understanding, and comprehension (Lower-Order Thinking Skills, or LOTS) and assignments, projects, and activities that require application, demonstration, analysis, synthesis, and evaluation (Higher-Order Thinking Skills, or HOTS).

Harking back to the battle, "Look It Up for a Report" versus "Inquiry Makes the Learning More Lasting," on which side would one find the lower-level thinking skills? The ubiquitous report is the answer. If all that a teacher requires of a youngster is to repeat facts found in a reference book, the student has no opportunity to develop his thinking skills. Students cannot be blamed for choosing an easy way if classroom teachers and school librarians do not offer constant guidance and evaluation. Preparing a report is as easy as copying and pasting. The report tells Who, What, Where, and When. Such questions imply there is no need to think, just transfer "the facts" to one's paper. The classroom teachers' requirement has been fulfilled.

That is where the Essential Question (EQ) comes in. The EQ can move the process from a mere "report" to an "inquiry." The inquiry requires HOTS. Students cannot answer EQ with a simple "yes" or "no." Neither can they copy and paste the "right answer." The EQ moves beyond the LOTS skills in favor of such questions as Why, What if, and How. Comparing and contrasting at the EQ level require students to look at the "supposed" answer(s) from varying angles. This entails good information seeking behaviors and strong search strategies. Who better to teach these skills than school librarians?

One must remember that students develop the skills in the same way that they learn any skills-based activity: repetition. The repetition can take on deeper dimensions over time. Retention does not happen instantaneously.

Hermann Ebbinghaus's work found that over half of any material learned is forgotten within an hour. Two-thirds is lost within a day. Retention does not decline much beyond that point. In other words, information retained for a day is knowledge that stays (Cherry, 2010).

Just as an athlete's prowess deepens and the athlete becomes more self-assured with his ability as he sees his development over time, students gain confidence in their ability to grasp concepts and create new expressions of their learning when guided by a collaborative effort between classroom teachers and school librarians.

Just as serious athletes do not expect overnight success, school librarians must not expect overnight success when experiencing systemic change. It is important to expect an achievement drop. As with some life experiences, things seem to get worse before they get better. Convincing classroom teachers and administration that research requires constant repetition to become a learned process, followed intuitively by the information seeker, could contribute to an achievement drop as well as a sense of failure, of frustration, and of incompleteness.

Inquiry-Based Learning: Collaboration and Student Dispositions

The affective component, not only that of students, but also that of classroom teachers, factors into the achievement drops. According to AASL (2009), dispositions toward teaching/learning guide intellectual behaviors. Convincing classroom teachers that repetitive use of research models can impact critical thinking and have bearing on state testing necessitates school librarians' active promotion of possible gains. School librarians should not overlook Keith Curry Lance's work on evidence-based practice (Lance, Welborn, & Hamilton-Pennell, 1993). Here one can find empirical data to support the work of school librarians in an inquiry-based teaching/learning environment.

Dispositions reflect the students' curiosity, flexibility, resilience, imagination, reflection, and self-evaluation. Having skills is not the same as using skills or doing something with skills. There is more to learning than *what* they learn; there are the *why* and the *how* of learning (AASL, 2009).

The Learning Wheel provided in Figure 1.2 shows the inquiry needed by both classroom teachers and students. Education has drawn heavily from public health's evidence-based approach. The wheel's questions work as well for students as for educators. However, study of the wheel will remind classroom teachers and school librarians that starting with a goal and writing objectives help solidify the direction, strategies, and activities needed for a successful inquiry-based unit of study.

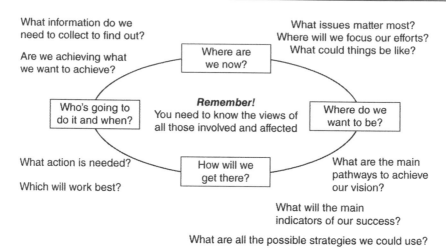

Figure 1.2 The Learning Wheel. *Source*: Roe (1995). Reprinted with permission.

It is challenging work. School librarians' focus on collaboration and its benefits for student achievement is new for some and not well practiced by many. As long as school librarians' "disposition" remains positive, willing, creative, and proactive, success is inevitable and attainable!

Chapter 2

Collaboration Overview

The Collaborative Approach

Collaboration, as defined by the *New World Dictionary of the American Language*, includes such key phrases as "working together" and "co-operation in some literary, artistic, or scientific undertaking" and *Roget's Thesaurus* calls it a "teaming up." Why are these essential to the full understanding of the definition? Is it because they connote the role of collaboration in the teaching/learning environment? Yes, whether the collaboration is between student and classroom teacher, student and student, student and school librarians, administration and faculty, or classroom teacher and school librarians.

Throughout the book, "school librarian" will be the nomenclature rather than "teacher librarian," "media specialist," or "library media specialist." The AASL Board of Directors, after many considerations, including a survey of the field, determined the professional title "school librarian" better reflects the roles of the 21st-century school library professional as a leader, instructional partner, information specialist, teacher, and program administrator.

Is collaboration a natural result within the teaching/learning community? Unfortunately, no. The theme of the March 2005 *Library Media Connection (LMC)* was "Invite Better Collaboration." That same year,

Peter Milbury (2005) published "Collaboration: Ten Important Reasons to Take It Seriously." Even earlier, *ERIC Digest* published Russell's article "Teachers and Librarian: Collaborative Relationships" (2000) that had an extensive bibliography to strong positional articles on the need for collaboration. Although evidence of a move toward collaborations between classroom teachers and school librarians dates back to mid-1990, collaboration has never gained the status of best practice.

Within traditional classrooms' focusing on state learning standards, classroom teachers allow students little collaborative time. True, they might include brief blogging, have group work for a period, or assign groups for outside work unstructured and unguided, fashioned only by the students' choices.

Is collaboration a natural result between or among classroom teachers? Actually, not as much as might be expected. A percentage of classroom teachers enjoy the autonomy the school's culture and their subjects allow. When they have their "free periods" or "released time," there is the endless paperwork to tackle, whether expected by the administration or imposed by the grading of homework. There are team meetings or department meetings for

1. setting long-term goals and objectives

2. reviewing tasks and progress toward those goals and objectives

3. strategizing ways to impact and/or modify the school's culture

How often has time for collaboration been on the agenda only to be supplanted by a more imminent issue?

Is collaboration a natural occurrence between classroom teachers and school librarians? Absolutely not, for four key reasons:

- Time

- Insufficient professional development

- Classroom teachers' lack of understanding about school librarians' curricular role

- School librarians' hesitancy to assume a leadership role

Classroom teachers' classic response to new initiatives is, "I don't have time. I have all of the standards to cover, too many papers to grade, lessons to plan, assigned responsibilities, and extra duties to perform." Collaboration provides valuable free time, enabling classroom teachers to concentrate on state standards, lesson planning, and content.

> "Often times I find myself wrapped up in the small day-to-day details of managing the classroom. Unfortunately, the big ideas get lost. Large projects become daunting tasks that I would rather avoid. Working with an effective school librarian opens up the

door for more effective lessons that create meaningful learning" (B. Andrews, personal communication, April 2, 2009).

In addition, classroom teachers feel pressure to incorporate technology without adequate skill development or training for instructional use. School librarians provide technological leadership for both students and classroom teachers. A true partnership forms when classroom teachers and school librarians are equally involved with the technology.

When school librarians put out the word that they would like to collaborate and ask the faculty "How can I help you?" most often nothing happens. Without a response, school librarians assume lack of interest. Classroom teachers might not know how to respond: What is the school librarian asking? What am I expected to do? How do we go about "sharing"? School librarians once spent their time behind the circulation desk or in their offices preparing orders. During the 1990s and early 2000s, theoreticians and some practitioners advocated a new collaborative role for school librarians. For many building educators and school librarians, this new view remains foreign in practice. Where is the professional development that could alleviate the awkwardness created by such a simple question: "How can I help you?"

A proactive approach to overcome perception necessitates at least the following three components:

1. *School librarians know the curriculum.* They have access to textbooks and curriculum maps. Curriculum maps, known as pacing guides or scope and sequence, give school librarians the big picture that allows approaching classroom teachers with collaborative suggestions. Collaboration is not happenstance, but deliberate and intentional.

    For each unit of study, each subject area, each grade, school librarians begin a short template of information crucial to successful collaboration. School librarians use online software to establish a series of folders indicating subjects and grades. When storing templates for each unit of study, school librarians avoid using teachers' names because of attrition and expansion and reduction of staff. When classes utilize the LMC for one of the study units, school librarians begin to fill in the template (see Figure 2.1) and to use a unit-of-study planning guide that school librarians and classroom teachers might share.

    As collaborations become more common, a natural evolution would be for classroom teachers and school librarians to modify the unit-of-study planning guide (see Figure 2.2), or to devise one unique to their unit expectation. Whatever outcome results, each unit of study includes school librarians' lesson plans for initiating and enhancing research and reviewing research skills. The *Standards for the 21st-Century Learner* (AASL, 2007) and the National Educational Technology Standards (NETS) from the International Society for Technology in Education (ISTE, 2010) are the essence of every lesson plan created by school librarians. Classroom teachers focus

Unit of Study

Gr.	Subject (e.g., Science)	Teacher	# of Students	Unit of Study— (e.g., Solar System)	MP or Q Marking Period or Quarter	# of Days	Primary Methods of Instruction (e.g., lecture or Power Point, or Smartboard, or Q & A, or Other)	Materials (e.g., text, video software program kits, Other	Organization e.g. Lggp/Ind (large group, independent, pairs, or Other)	Final Product MULTI-MODAL (must have at least two different inputs to be multimodal, such as sound, images, photos, text, students' own words, student drawings); could use Photo Story, Animoto, a new free Web 2.0 tool (No PPT!)

Figure 2.1 Curriculum Map Template.

Grade: _____	Number of Sections: _____
Subject: _____	
Unit: _____	Number of Students: _____
Teacher: _____	
General Description of Assignment:	Total Periods of Instruction: _____
_____	
_____	Calendar Quarter: _____
Level of Instruction:	
Introduced	**Assignment Output(s):**
Reinforced	(Could combine traditional with
Expanded	authentic)
Comment: _____	Test
_____	Observation
	Written critique
Materials:	Oral report
Text	Physical project
Print resources	Digital project
Digital sources_____	Describe briefly (attach any handouts):
Organization of Instruction:	_____
Large group	_____
Groups of 3–5	_____
Pairs	_____
Individual	
Primary Teaching Methods:	**Objectives for the Assignment:**
Computer-based	_____
Desk work	_____
Lecture	_____
Discussion	_____
Independent study	**Key Activities and Strategies:**
Programmed (incl. learning stations)	1. _____
Project	2. _____
Comment: _____	3. _____
_____	**AASL Standards for the 21st Century**
National and/or State Technology	**Learner:**
Standards:	_____
_____	_____
_____	_____
_____	_____
State Content Standards:	**Additional Notes:**
_____	_____
_____	_____
_____	_____

Figure 2.2 Unit-of-Study Planning Guide.

From *Collaborating for Inquiry-Based Learning: School Librarians and Teachers Partner for Student Achievement* by Virginia L. Wallace and Whitney Norwood Husid. Santa Barbara, CA: Libraries Unlimited. Copyright © 2011.

on lessons, activities, and strategies related to state learning standards for students while school librarians align both the AASL standards and NETS to the state standards pertinent to the unit of study.

2. *School librarians seek out classroom teachers who think "out of the box."* It takes more than one's observation of actions and responses to determine where there might be a kindred educator. But that observation helps school librarians to decide from which collection to draw when making one's appeal "to try a partnership." With knowledge of one's collection and of the class' upcoming units of study, school librarians choose a unit that the collection supports well. With that knowledge, school librarians make their approach. The specificity with which school librarians connect with classroom teachers builds teachers' confidence that collaboration might lead to greater student achievement. It is the old theory that two heads are better than one.

3. *School librarians ask to be on committees and participate in meetings that directly impact the role of the LMC.* Offering input at curriculum meetings and demonstrating new technological tools at faculty meetings emphasize information literacy and the centrality of the LMC to the educational process.

Some school librarians hesitate to approach classroom teachers without clear-cut administrative support. Overwhelmed by clerical, managerial, and custodial duties of the LMC, they passively respond with lists of appropriate books and websites to classroom teachers' requests for support. Usually, such unwillingness to assert themselves for the benefit of students' academic growth can unfavorably impact classroom teachers' response to "How can I help you?" Being 21st-century leaders requires school librarians to leave their comfort zone and accept the challenge of collaboration. Without outreach, no collaboration can develop.

Synergy of Purpose

Collaboration cannot occur alone. When two or more educators pool purposes and talents, collaboration might happen. Sometimes, cooperation passes for collaboration. Sometimes, coordination is assumed to be collaboration. Sometimes, educators equate consensus with collaboration. In actuality, collaboration takes all of them along with commitment and compromise. There is synergy of purpose. The whole is greater than the sum of its parts and greater than any individual component.

Cooperation cannot be collaboration, for to cooperate is merely to respect one another's ideas and to acquiesce if necessary. It does not demand the investment required by collaboration. Collaboration will not happen, however, without cooperation.

Coordination does not need two or more to be engaged. One can coordinate alone so that others benefit from the planning, aligning, and strategizing. Educators admire those who coordinate well, whether activities, schedules, or strategies. It does not mean they embrace collaboration.

"I'm not in favor. However, I will not stand in the way. I will not sabotage the agreement made by all." Such is consensus, which cannot have any "no" votes (no thumbs down). Consensus commits everyone to the project but not always to a common vision. With collaboration, shared objectives and shared processes achieve the goal.

Best Practice

If the goal is student achievement, students need to help in the management of what they learn and how. The 1980s' pedagogy stressed that learning takes place when students understand the purpose (objective[s]). More than 20 years later, the educational trends state that teachers will practice the following:

- Clarify the expectation(s) (goal).

- Show the students a way (process) to reach those expectations.

- State the steps (objectives) necessary within the process to reach the goal.

- Expect student success and give guidance to assure that success (rubrics and formative assessment).

- Make possible diverse opportunities for individual students to find their best method for learning (activities/strategies).

- Correlate the teaching and learning with a final demonstration or demonstrations of what one has learned (assessments).

The recommended means for showing skill development, increased literacy, and knowledge-base gain would be through creative expression: a critical thinking level of Bloom's Taxonomy. For the teaching/learning experience to include student synthesis, the summative assessment focuses on construction of new learning. The 21st-century learner produces something to spotlight what he gained. Technology holds the key. It is impossible to conceive of today's student devoid of technology's influence. Since the ubiquitous computer in today's school symbolizes acceptance of its instructional role, use of educational software and free Internet programs gives students breadth and depth of expression. Tight budgets open Web 2.0 portals for school librarians, classroom teachers, and students. Many Web 2.0 applications have proven track records as witnessed by the plethora of blogs, websites, video postings, and worldwide communities among school-age children.

Within a collaborative unit of study, teaching practices listed above reinforce putting students at the helm of their learning experiences.

"The question should be what's worth learning. The trouble is that this very important question is not asked nearly often enough. Discourse around education tends to be about method. How are we going to get students to learn what we think they ought to learn? We should instead educate for the unknown, for what might come up, for nimble ways of thinking about it, for large understandings. . . . To me that means that ninety percent of what we teach is a waste of time. . . . Curriculum is one of the most resistant fronts of education" (Perkins as cited in Newell, 2010).

The collaboration between classroom teachers and school librarians represents a holistic effort to make students the engineers of their own learning. They build upon the scaffolding created by master constructors—classroom teachers and school librarians. The process eliminates ambiguity: problem solving versus problems. Student anticipation of success and their behaviors controlled by their own commitment to the challenge guide them through the uncertainties that could be problems, but in contrast are problem solving. Because of their involvement in the process and their resolve to attain success outlined via a rubric, students strengthen their learning and outcomes are no longer negligible.

Skills, Dispositions, Responsibilities, Self-Assessment

An old road map for teacher effectiveness holds relevance for today's students who take responsibility for their learning. Rather than a classroom in which students are passive recipients of lectures and teacher-constructed learning, the road map engages the student. The students' engagement parallels their new attitudes toward this affective learning.

- Get their attention.

- Lay a path before them that they can follow.

- Put up road signs to guide them along the way.

- Offer a rest stop for review and reflection.

- Offer impetus (increased speed limit) through challenges and stimulations.

The road map should concentrate on students' skills, dispositions, responsibilities, and self-assessment, covered in *Standards for the 21st-Century Learner in Action* (AASL, 2009). School librarians and classroom teachers build collaborative units of study that target *skills* (technology, constructivism), *dispositions* (attitudes and ethical behaviors), *responsibilities* (rubric challenges, inquiry learning, higher-order thinking/critical thinking), and *self-assessment* (reflection, personal growth, summative assessment).

Every collaborative step embeds AASL standards into the students' learning activities and authentic learning situations. Readers will see the footprints of the four 21st-century student foci in each collaborative component. AASL's work from *Information Power* (1998) to *Standards for the 21st-Century Learner in Action* (2009) influences the meaning and implementation of collaboration in the teaching/learning environment. Not only does collaboration increase student achievement, but also the LMCs' and school librarians' worth.

Chapter 3

Prior Knowledge

The Beginning of Inquiry-Based Learning

Is prior knowledge what we once knew but have forgotten? No! Is prior knowledge stored for future use? Yes! It is recalled information. Prior knowledge is a scaffolding tool. A student uses his prior knowledge to build his new knowledge. Prior knowledge lies dormant until making a correlation between what was learned and what is new learning. Each learner mentally "holds individual experiences and has formed knowledge based on those experiences. The premise of education, therefore, is to take the experience of the child into account and to help the child construct new knowledge or to reconstruct preexisting erroneous knowledge" (A. Beach, personal communication, 2010).

All learners like to test their prior knowledge from time to time. How much was remembered? Why can't it be recalled? How does one get it back? What are some tricks for remembering certain things? Why do some have better recollection than others? According to Ebbinghaus' Forgetting Curve, educators can expect that half of what students take with them from class is forgotten within the first hour (Cherry, 2010). That fact increases the importance of allowing students opportunities to stretch their memories and solidify their knowledge and understanding of academic materials presented.

Assimilation and Accommodation

Typically, educators equate stretching memories and solidifying knowledge with assimilation. However, in Jean Piaget's adaptive process, there is both assimilation and accommodation. These intellectual adaptations can occur simultaneously and complementarily. Students' learning assimilation and accommodation can function together and create balance. The processes are concurrent and in concert with one another. Consider a teaching scenario with a school librarian who asks a question or presents a puzzling situation. The students take in the experience created by the problem and assimilate it with existing cognitive structures. The assimilation transforms the problem from its original definition into the learners' mental schema (Piaget & Barbel, 1969). Simultaneous with the assimilation is the accommodation: cognitive structure adjusts to external reality. The process of adaptation modifies both structure of knowledge and external reality (Bybee & Sund, 1982).

Piaget's theory supports the idea that to build on one's prior knowledge, one must assimilate and accommodate. The adaptation, both assimilation and accommodation, of one's cognitive structure (his prior knowledge) offers a balance between internal and external factors (Piaget & Barbel, 1969). Thus, educators who follow Jean Piaget believe a developmentally appropriate curriculum that emphasizes the critical role of students' experiences and interactions with the environment enhances students' logical and conceptual growth (Bybee & Sund, 1982).

School librarians with this awareness recognize the futility of introducing a new concept that they have not first tied to the students' prior experiences and knowledge. School librarians in their teaching must realize the role object permanence plays in establishing cognitive structures. In today's rapidly changing and instantly connected world, mere regurgitation of facts will not give the learner a competitive edge in the global job market. By studying the student culture of one's school, school librarians can discover what knowledge the students possess before jumping into steps of research that assume the students are following the process.

Focusing on students' needs when collaborating with classroom teachers offers a team approach to the unit of study. Taking into account ethnicity, boy/girl ratio, attitudes about school and about themselves, state test scores, and past academic records helps classroom teachers and school librarians to set goals, write objectives, plan activities, strategize, develop helpful rubrics, and establish assessments.

When prior knowledge melds with present learning, one can expect students' current understandings to remain active and viable and eventually to become prior knowledge for future learning explorations. In the circular continuum, school librarians allow students to find answers and guide them toward those answers when clarity is questionable. According to *Standards for the 21st Century Learner in Action* (AASL, 2009), school librarians "are in an ideal position in each school to address the needs and to develop the abilities and attitudes of the whole child, not just the student's academic performance on specified content" (p. 6). This means that in whatever they are teaching, whether using research techniques or locating materials, they are shaping students' commitment to lifelong learning and reading.

Differentiation

It should be the goal of all classroom teachers and all school librarians to seek innovative and constantly changing ways to evaluate students' needs. Besides knowing that prior knowledge is a key to student need, there is the complexity created by population diversity. Students benefit from differentiated instruction when based on their prior knowledge. Differentiation is the idea and practice that any teacher can reach and challenge students if finding the proper instruction and motivation are important to the teacher (Tomlinson, 2001). With knowledge about students' needs, classroom teachers can group them flexibly by willingness, interests, and learning styles. It is in these groups that students will receive instruction in both small-group or individual settings. Whole-group instruction may occur, but it is no longer the only utilized method of delivery. Classroom teachers ask each student the same questions, which are essential to their understanding of the concept, but allow the students to learn in ways that meet individual needs. Key to differentiation is teachers' assuming responsibility for adjusting instruction according to students' specific needs. Following a predetermined skill sequence may not match students' learning methods (Walker-Dalhouse et al., 2009). Differentiated instruction requires individualizing learning by arranging the classroom and the entire school for small-group, large-group, and individual learning. Classroom teachers, school librarians, and students alike assume accountability for the learning with an expectation of a continual learning process and practice.

Given that school librarians are responsible for teaching information literacy standards both within the LMC and in classrooms, best practice is to differentiate lessons in order to meet the learning needs of all students. Collaboration between school librarians and classroom teachers enables differentiated instruction and increases student achievement. Hence, ongoing professional development is critical if classroom teachers and school librarians expect to implement differentiation. Professional development providers must demonstrate differentiation and provide advice, constructive criticism, and ideas if needed (H. Burdette, personal communication, January 2010).

John Dewey, a champion of experiential (progressive) education, wanted classroom teachers to understand that what they taught had to reflect their pupils' different past experiences (V&A Museum of Childhood, 2010). Familial ties, whether viewed by outsiders as healthy or unhealthy, are a child's anchor. A child might have a problem with a positive response to researching why the Apaches attacked military forts when his home condition distracts and dissuades his participation. The more students can discern their own place on the learning hierarchy, the more likely they are to take responsibility for strengthening past learning and tackling new learning.

Using the KWHL Chart

One tool found useful for directing student thinking toward earlier learning exposures and how they come to know is the KWHL chart. The **K** of the chart is "What do I **Know**?" Here students reflect on knowledge learned earlier: What percent have they retained? What can they recall? What value did they place on that learning experience? What has each brought forward as the foundation for new learning?

Developing self-awareness about one's learning is not "What do I think I know?" not "Why do I care what I know?" and not "Who needs to know?" but "*What do I know?*" Each time a student willingly assumes the role of self-examiner, the more capable he becomes as a well-rounded student. What he knows might come from memorization or from mimicking what he has heard without understanding. He may infer from his "knowing" and he may compare his learning. Each "knowing" act gives classroom teachers and school librarians insight into that student's needs.

When a student asks "What do I know?" he studies his own personal road map or at least, its early developing stages. If classroom teachers guide him along his road map, current knowledge morphs into prior knowledge, and the cycle continues. The student ultimately evolves into a lifelong learner. He reaches the **L** of the KWHL: what he has learned. "What I have Learned," attained many times throughout a child's education, converts to the **K** and the process begins afresh: "What do I **Know**?"

To span from K to L, two other questions work in partnership with "What do I **Know**: What do I **Want** to know?" and "**How** do I find the answers?" "What do I want to know" arises from Essential Questions (EQ) of the unit of study and creates the research need. The questions within the big question must challenge the student's reasoning: his deductive powers, such as what if, how, why, compare, and contrast. The inquiry-based questions lead the student into a research mode with print and nonprint references. Through trial and error and site evaluations, the student determines which resources best help him answer the overriding questions within his research.

Inquiry-based learning allows students to take ownership for finding answers, with guidance from classroom teachers and school librarians who are responsible for teaching a process for inquiry discovery. The students' information seeking behaviors and skills need constant nurturing, guidance, and expansion.

The **H** presupposes an overriding position because without knowledge of "How to find the answers," students approach the research process without an important piece for success. Prior knowledge supports the "How" of the KWHL. With prior knowledge, the student evaluates his sources and selects the ones most propitious for the task at hand. The student carries out the research process utilizing a research model most appropriate for the task. Research models vary as widely as the diverse populations they serve.

And so, at the end of the KWHL where prior knowledge acts as anchor, students move from what they know to what they want to know, how they are to find it, and lastly, what they learned. As part of the "What did I learn," students evaluate and reflect. Classroom teachers and school librarians evaluate and reflect. Collaboration among students, among classroom teachers, between school librarians and classroom teachers, and between school librarians and students mirror pedagogically best practices.

> Does public education allow time for such theoretical positioning? Therein lies the problem.

With a plethora of choices for teaching in the educational arena, too many classroom teachers have buried themselves within bureaucratic folly rather than creating an experiential setting to foster student depth and breadth of learning. The pressure to have all students at the same level of learning creates stifled work environments and does not allow time for students to construct their learning. Students who have chances to build their knowledge retain more because they have had not only sufficient time, but also multiple involvements with the study topic. If classroom teachers and school librarians engage in what students are doing and use students' prior knowledge as the new learning catalyst, classroom teachers, school librarians, and students will leave the experience wiser, academically grounded, and collaboratively stronger.

Chapter 4

Essential Questions and Inquiry-Based Learning

The Inquiry Foundation

If, as Cushman (1989) states in her seminal article "Asking Essential Questions: Curriculum Development," the goal of education is for students to engage their minds and think well, questions need to organize the curriculum. Questions propel thinking, whereas answers often stifle it. The right kinds of questions stimulate more questions; thought continues as inquiry (Elder & Paul, 2005).

> Inquiry is the process of seeking knowledge, raising questions, searching for answers, evaluating information, and asking new questions based on new understandings.

Because the knowledge base for all disciplines is constantly expanding and the fund of knowledge is ever increasing, developing the skills and dispositions necessary for lifelong learning is more important than mastering soon-to-be-outdated content. Inquiry-based learning emphasizes skill development and encourages dispositions and behaviors that enable lifelong learning. Epitomized by *Standards for the 21st-Century Learner in Action* (AASL, 2009) and supported by essential questions (EQ) (see Table 4.1), inquiry-based learning shifts the classroom focus from teaching to learning.

Table 4.1 AASL Standards and Essential Questions

AASL Standards	Essential Questions
Excerpted from *Standards for the 21st-Century Learner* by the American Association of School Librarians, a division of the American Library Association, copyright © 2007 American Library Association. Available for download at www.ala.org/aasl/standards. Used with permission.	
1.1.2 Use prior and background knowledge as context for new learning. 1.1.3 Develop and refine a range of questions to frame the search for new understanding.	Essential questions and current knowledge guide students toward questions for investigation and inquiry.
1.2.5 Demonstrate adaptability by changing the inquiry focus, questions, resources, or strategies when necessary to achieve success.	Essential questions are revisited as understanding, circumstances, or knowledge changes over time.
1.3.2 Seek divergent perspectives during information gathering and assessment. 2.3.2 Consider diverse perspectives in drawing conclusions. 4.4.4 Interpret new information based on cultural and social context.	Essential questions encourage the use of multiple perspectives and are interdisciplinary in nature.
2.3.1 Connect understanding to the real world. 3.1.5 Connect learning to community issues. 3.3.4 Create products that apply to authentic, real-world contexts.	Essential questions are relevant over time, focus on important issues, and connect learning with personal experience. Essential questions foster authentic learning.
4.1.4 Seek information for personal learning in variety of formats and genres. 4.2.1 Display curiosity by pursuing interests through multiple resources. 4.3.3 Seek opportunities for pursuing personal and aesthetic growth.	Essential questions promote lifelong learning. Essential questions reappear throughout one's life.

Student questions rather than teacher lessons drive inquiry-based learning. Helping students determine what they want to know and what they are motivated to learn, classroom teachers and school librarians act as coaches, guides, or facilitators. The excitement generated when children study their own questions moves them along the continuum from LOTS (memorizing the facts) to HOTS (creating a solution to a real-world problem). Particularly well suited for collaborative learning projects, inquiry-based learning validates students' experiences and prior knowledge.

Thus, curriculum planning begins with the question "What do students know about the topic?" Wise classroom teachers and school librarians do not bore students with facts or information already mastered. Nor do they attempt to teach new information or skills not grounded in students' prior knowledge. Some questions posed by school librarians and classroom teachers act as foundational questions. These questions are just that—the basis for the next level of learning. Foundational questions are fact finders. They identify who, what, where, and when. These questions, referred to as supporting or formational, form the necessary path and structure for what will be presented next.

Aware of curricular standards from current and previous school years, classroom teachers and school librarians use fact finders and identifiers to elicit students' knowledge. KWHL provides a framework for this discussion. While taking notes on the board (perhaps creating a mind map), classroom teachers promote students' involvement by asking them to share their knowledge and experiences with the topic. Based on this discussion, classroom teachers and school librarians guide students toward creating questions about what they want to know or investigate. They help students make connections to and build on each other's ideas. Their questions become the basis for classroom activities, information searches, and inquiry as the focus shifts to how to find answers. Using a research model to structure the search, students evaluate and select resources based on prior knowledge, current understanding, and information goals. Building on questioning and searching, authentic student-created projects culminate in generating new knowledge. As the final, but recursive step, students evaluate what they learned, how they learned, and what they need or want to learn as the process continues.

Essential Questions Explored

Ideally, classroom teachers and school librarians have essential questions (EQ) in mind as they guide students' exploration and direct their inquiry. But what exactly are essential questions? Why are they important? How do they contribute to student learning and the development of critical thinking skills? EQ address big ideas that remain significant over time (Bush, 2009)—ideas with which scholars, philosophers, and ordinary people have grappled since the beginning of time. Often the subject of novels, plays, artistic works, and philosophical debate, they are not easy to answer. In fact, they may not have an answer or may have more than one answer, depending on time, circumstance, or nature of the questioner. Their importance is based not on obtaining an answer, but on the quest for understanding to which these questions lead. By concentrating on important issues, ideas, or concerns, EQ address archetypal themes. Essential questions

> touch our hearts and souls. They are central to our lives. They help to define what it means to be human. . . . Essential questions usually probe the deep and often confounding issues confronting us—complex and baffling matters that elude simple answers: Life-Death-Marriage-Identity-Purpose-Betrayal-Honor Integrity-Courage. (McKenzie, 2005)

All of the following practical examples explore EQ characteristics and their relationship to curriculum and critical thinking skills:

- What is humankind's relationship with nature? What should it be?

- How did the universe begin?

- Does life exist elsewhere in the universe?

- What is man's responsibility to his fellow men?

- What is a friend?

These questions address big ideas that are meaningful and consequential. They require more than yes or no; they require deep thought, analysis, and evaluation, and cannot be answered with simple facts. They are interdisciplinary. Consequently, the question of mankind's relationship with nature can be explored within the disciplines:

- Science: Consider the issues of global warming, the destruction of the rain forests, and the plight of endangered species.

- Literature: The Romantic poets Wordsworth and Coleridge explore man's relationship with nature in their poems *Tintern Abbey* and *Rime of the Ancient Mariner*.

- Social Studies: How has man's need for raw materials contributed to empire building and colonization? What is the economic impact of recycling and green technologies?

- Math: What are the mathematical models for population growth? What variables might impact these models?

EQ form the basis for curriculum because essential questions are central to all other questions (McKenzie, 2005). They organize the curriculum unit, a semester-long or year-long course, or a cross-curricular collaboration. Unit questions derived from EQ provide entry points into the curriculum. For a high-school English literature class, application of the essential question "What is humankind's relationship with nature?" results in the following unit questions:

- How did the Romantic poets view man's relationship with nature? Compare and contrast this with the classical view.

- How does Wordsworth describe his relationship with nature in *Tintern Abbey?*

- How has his relationship with nature changed over time? Predict how it might change if he were to visit the abbey a third time.

- How does Coleridge view nature in *Rime of the Ancient Mariner?*

- How does Coleridge's view challenge Wordworth's?

- Which author most typifies the Romantic view of nature, and why?

- Speculate how Wordsworth or Coleridge might react to mankind's current relationship with nature.

Functions of Essential Questions (EQ)

EQ connect learning with personal experience. They foster authentic learning because students recognize their importance and see the issues at work in their own lives. Children can relate to the question of man's relationship with nature. They care about polar bears and rain-forest creatures. They enjoy hiking, swimming, and camping. They see the effects of pollution on waterways, air, and neighborhoods.

EQ encourage multiple perspectives (Brown, 2009). People with distinct backgrounds, experiences, and priorities view the same problem differently. People in developed countries consider the long-term effects of global warming a priority, whereas those in third-world countries are more immediately concerned about malaria and clean drinking water. Based on their religious and ethnic backgrounds, children's understandings of their relationships with nature vary.

Crossing disciplines and encouraging multiple perspectives, EQ allow students to approach the same topic from their unique multiple intelligences (Gardner, 2006). Students possessed of linguistic intelligence may choose to explore man's relationship with nature through literature, whereas students with spatial intelligence may prefer to create models or charts. Students with strong intrapersonal skills may keep journals, while students with interpersonal intelligence may form a recycling club or organize a school-wide Earth Day celebration.

EQ encourage development and use of critical thinking skills. Students actively participate and do not passively receive information to regurgitate on tests. EQ necessitate action, such as deciding, defining, or predicting, that requires students to move beyond knowledge to higher levels of Bloom's Revised Taxonomy: apply, analyze, evaluate, and create (Anderson & Krathwohl, 2001). Actions associated with EQ include but are not limited to the following:

- Conceive or formulate
- Speculate

- Choose

- Problem solve

- Argue

- Test

- Imagine

- Investigate

- Prove or disprove

- Calculate

- Discover

- Appraise

None of the above functions merely fact find. Stafford (2009) classifies questions by purpose and distinguishes between supporting and essential questions. Supporting questions, known as foundational or formational, include closed, yes/no, and fact-finding queries. EQ are open; they require sense-making and judgment-forming. Students must sort, judge, and critique. They must clarify, compare and contrast, or infer. All of these actions represent analysis, synthesis, and evaluation, the top three levels on Bloom's Taxonomy. The chart in Figure 4.1, adapted from Stafford (2009), schematically presents

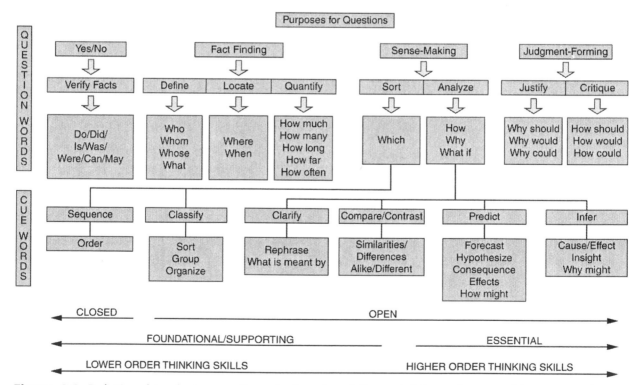

Figure 4.1 Relationships between Foundational and Essential Questions and Lower- and Higher-Order Thinking Skills. *Source*: Adapted from Stafford (2009).

the relationships between foundational and essential questions and lower- and higher-order thinking skills.

Elder and Paul (2005) note that superficial questions lead to superficial understanding, and unclear questions lead to unclear understanding.

Essential questions lead to lifelong learning because they are never fully answered. They change as understanding evolves, experience progresses, and new ideas arise, not only in school but throughout life.

Inquiry advances as students engage higher-order thinking skills and demonstrate increasingly sophisticated information seeking behaviors. A sound research model guides the information search and allows students to achieve newer and deeper understanding.

Chapter 5

Information Seeking Behaviors

Understanding Information Seeking Behaviors

"Information seeking behaviors" is a phrase new to countless public-school educators; it lacks an identity concrete in the minds of those who work with students. It needs a definitive understanding, however, because classroom teachers and school librarians guide students' work with essential questions (EQ) and inquiry-based learning more successfully when they can associate information seeking behaviors with their students.

Seeking versus Searching

The research defines differently "seeking" and "searching." "Seeking" means hunting for, looking for, and trying to find. "Searching" means investigating and exploring. The two words have both connotative and denotative meanings; and even though it would seem the definitions of both denote the same, the terms connote differently. Students seek what they do not know. Unsure of what they need or want or the method for locating information, students look around to find something acceptable. When looking around, they omit print because they lack skill with tables of content and indexes. Instead, they google a topic; they surf the web. The web provides busyness without any meaningful results. The surfing takes time and produces a plethora of URL hits used by students in the order of rank on the page. Students lack clarity for meaningful research. Thus, they seek and cannot explain the dissonant feeling about what they are doing and how they respond to what they are doing.

When students search, they have a target. They know a topic they must investigate. Classroom teachers and school librarians either have given the assignment without specific direction or have allowed students to choose a topic of interest. Such loose directives immediately create an information seeking behavior predicated on anxiety or fear of failure. Students, knowing so little about the subject field, appear to enjoy such freedom; in actuality, they do not know where to begin. Because students lack good information seeking strategies, the "search" morphs into another "seek."

"Just this week, I experienced once again the frustration of a student who is given an obscure individual to write a report about. One of the DOE staffers gave me the name of an inventor that her 6-year-old niece was to report on. After one hour of surfing and checking online as well as print resources the only information I could find was that yes, this person had invented the dustpan and I located a picture of the patent but no biographical information on the inventor could be found. If I was frustrated, I hesitate to think how the student was feeling. This situation reminded me of how important it is for teachers to collaborate with their library media specialist before making assignments. We too often see the results of frustrated students seeking to fulfill unrealistic assignments. We must continue to recruit teachers and administrators to understand and to become advocates for us as instructional partners for the academic success of our children" (Makela, 2003).

Attitudes and Behaviors

With either an assigned or a "free choice" topic, students take with them into the process certain attitudes and behaviors. These attitudes and behaviors are as diverse as the student body. This is where the work of classroom teachers and school librarians must focus. How are they to know the multitude of student feelings and reactions? Since they cannot, and since it would be impossible to try, classroom teachers and school librarians must, instead, understand the following:

- What are the most common information seeking behaviors?
- How can classroom teachers and school librarians guide students through these attitudes to a better, clearer, more self-actualizing personal space when "searching"?
- What are some strategies to use when barriers arise?
- How often must those strategies be used?
- Where can one find support for expected behaviors and effective strategies?

• What are the differences/similarities in information seeking behaviors from primary to intermediate to high school?

Because this pursuit involves looking at what makes one person respond but not another, and all the ramifications of those responses or lack thereof, studying information seeking behaviors becomes complex. This complexity is created by students' differing responses to extrinsic and intrinsic stimuli. The following overview can provide the basis for expected behaviors when pursuing inquiry-based learning, using research models, and evaluating one's participation in the process.

The *Standards for the 21st-Century Learner in Action* (AASL, 2009) defines dispositions as "Ongoing beliefs and attitudes that guide thinking and intellectual behavior that can be measured through actions taken" (p. 12). "That can be measured through actions taken" are the operative words. When working with students and their approaches to finding answers, classroom teachers and school librarians need ways to measure, through students' actions, the progress they are making from lower-order thinking skills to higher-order skills. Bloom's Taxonomy reflects one's willingness to grow intellectually and cognitively. Measurement methods include rubrics, formative and summative assessments, and students' reflection. Tactics to support preparation for measurement are conducive study environments, needs assessment, prior knowledge, clear direction, educator guidance, and development of activities to appeal to varied learning styles.

Positive and Negative Challenges

The needs assessment, as a view of the learners' experiences, identifies areas of teaching/learning challenge. The challenges can be both positive and negative. A student with a history of academic and/or social failure will carry into the new teaching/learning environment a resistance to change. It is understandable that if one has fallen short multiple times, he will show reluctance for new undertakings. Rather than attempting to slough off the stigma, he embraces it by negatively approaching his task. Students with this mindset believe their intelligence is "simply fixed ... they have a certain amount and that's that" (Dweck, 2009).

Dweck's research "has shown that when students have a fixed mindset, they value looking smart over learning. They do not care to explore topics in depth; they are not [as] disposed to engage in critical thinking to gain and share knowledge; and they are low[er] on self-accountability and self-assessment strategies. In fact, rather than trying to recognize their weaknesses, they run from them, conceal them, and even lie about them" (p. 9).

If peer ridicule has occurred, the information seeking behavior represents further academic and social stigmatizing. The attitude becomes "I don't care," and the "seeking" is less than productive.

What tools do students need? They need openness to growth: a willingness to seek new learning, develop learning strategies, and engage in honest assessment of their strengths and weaknesses. How can school librarians cultivate the growth mindset? Foster it by praising students for their learning process and not for their intelligence. Praising intelligence leaves students vulnerable to plummeting confidence, motivation, and performance when the material becomes difficult (Dweck, 2009).

A different type of challenge might be the student who had strong guidance for early inquiry and anticipates the process. A zealous student can intimidate other learners if classroom teachers and school librarians do not channel the student's energy and output. Such students can benefit the overall information seeking experience or monopolize the teachers' attention.

Carol Kuhlthau's (2010) work on information seeking behaviors addresses physical and cognitive behaviors: attitudes, feelings, thoughts, and actions. Examples in the previous paragraphs are nothing new to educators, but addressing them in relation to information seeking is. Kuhlthau's Information Search Process (ISP) model examines closely when, where, and how students respond to research. ISP, a constructivist view of learning, includes the following stages:

- Initiating research assignments

- Selecting topics

- Exploring information

- Formulating focus

- Collecting information

- Preparing to present

- Assessing the process

Each stage further explores anxieties and attitudes students may experience during the research process. Problems intensify when school librarians do not reinforce research stages each time students use resources, whether print or nonprint.

Behaviors and attitudes prevalent among 20 to 30 untrained, unstructured classroom students encumber student patrons' development of library media skills. Possibly there should be a paradigm shift to (or at least a concentrated look at) conforming library services to user expectations.

> When students lack search initiative and resist finding answers, have classroom teachers and school librarians sought student input in order to understand the lack of motivation? One response is that lack of time dictates the answer is "No."

Classroom Culture

Another probable answer is that students do not understand the place called "library." They perceive the library as a place for finding a book for fun. Thus, for a certain percentage who do not like to read, they obviously do not like the library media center (LMC). If it involves reading, it cannot be a good place. For those who like to read, their questions are "Why aren't we hearing a story?" and "Why do I feel uneasy about being here? I can't follow this new purpose."

Once school librarians introduce new skills and techniques, they will discover a variety of research habits manifested. Not only are the reading populations varied, but so are the academic disciplines. Each class, each grade, each subject brings its own unique personality. The interdependence of activity, concept, and culture defines the ways in which students learn. Not only does school culture influence learning, but also students bring their own traditions into the classroom environment. The culture of the classroom, where students spend 180 days a year, adds to the individual's preconceived notion of what the LMC is and why students should go there. Some affective components of the classroom culture are age level, maturity, ethnicity, gender, homogeneous versus heterogeneous grouping, and special talents. Classroom teachers' response to learning styles and multiple intelligences directly affects lesson planning and activities and influences how students behave as a class and as individuals outside the classroom. Have they been allowed to be active participants, or have they been passive receivers?

If students are thrown in a situation in which their learning is more their responsibility than teacher-mandated, they initially exhibit confusion, anxiety, and/or reluctance. For instance, students do not come packaged with an intuitive sense concerning the ethical use of materials and resources. In an age of situational ethics, students witness unethical transactions and actions condoned, accepted, or tolerated. Since observation is one of life's most influential methods for learning, students see nothing wrong with plagiarism or copyright infringement if no one gets hurt. "Ethical behavior in the use of information must be taught. In this increasingly global world of information, students must be taught to seek diverse perspectives, gather and use information ethically, and use social tools responsibly and safely" (AASL, 2007).

Although given usage responsibility, students cannot be expected to have or understand this responsibility in an age flooded with information. A friend has a song the buddy likes—why not download from iPod to iPod? An online photograph is exactly what a student needs—what is wrong with copying it? Sites sell subject-area research papers—why not buy one, since the time saved could be useful elsewhere? Do not ask for permission; ask for forgiveness if necessary. Web-based research and social networking require understanding of netiquette and information-property rights for students to demonstrate respect, integrity, and ethical behavior. Classroom teachers and school librarians must continue to help students understand issues of right and wrong in the complex world of global information.

LMC Techniques

Since the LMC is the school's largest classroom, what techniques transfer well from the classroom to the LMC?

- *Nonlinguistic representations*: Because students are less likely to "cut and paste," use of concept maps and graphic organizers reduces plagiarism. Nonlinguistic representations encourage student synthesis and creativity.

- *Cooperative learning (group work)*: For example, students maintain Google Docs or drop.io where they learn how respectfully to share, modify, proofread, add, and/or delete one another's input as part of a collaborative team.

- *Venn diagrams*: Students make connections, such as how things are similar and/or different, vital analogies for moving to new learning and experiences (Marzano, Pickering & Pollock, 2001).

Information Seeking on the Web

Classroom teachers and school librarians employ the same stimuli and information organization when teaching students web research specifically. Although the expression "Students know more about technology than I ever will" floats among parents, classroom teachers, and school librarians, in practice, students require guidance through the plethora of web information. Being able to access thousands of sites is not equivalent to understanding and converting the information to knowledge.

Students may appear confident and verbalize that confidence, although a skills assessment might indicate otherwise (Hadro, 2010). From the 1999 study of high schoolers' information seeking behaviors (Fidel et al., 1999) to today's observation of students' reaction to inquiry-based learning, students manifest the same behaviors:

- Preference for searching versus using a web directory

- Reliance on past successful search experiences

- Use of safe and familiar websites

- Satisfaction with results but impatience with slow system retrieval responses.

A familiar and favored website is Google.com. Time and usage have failed to prove Google as a false or supportive aid (Hadro, 2010). And why the Google dilemma? In what way does it affect students' information seeking behaviors? For one thing, students see their teachers googling as an expedient means to find answers; yet their classroom teachers and school librarians tell them not to rely solely on Google but to seek comparative sources. Although the contradiction creates confusing student thoughts and behaviors, the required process leads to a more dynamic experience critical for moving student learners along a continuum from lower- to higher-order thinking skills.

Idle surfing inhibits sound student information seeking habits. When given broad, inconclusive directions for completing research assignments, after spending what they feel is adequate time on the computer, students often select the first hits returned without using evaluative criteria, such as relevance, authority, currency, and validity. Ironically, classroom teachers limit dedicated research time because of performance pressure on state standards tests. Language ability is ignored in the process. There is a relationship between language ability and formulation of information requests. Because most information on the web is as text, language comprehension is fundamental. Deciding which text to use, reading that text, using the content of the findings, and relating the information to one's search needs involve language comprehension—more than decoding words.

Educators' Involvement with the Whole Student

Attitude reflects aptitude; aptitude reflects attitude. If school librarians and classroom teachers design learning experiences that activate reading responses based on higher-order thinking skills and guide students through the exercises rather than leaving them to their own devises, language ability will improve. The saying "guide on the side" works for educators as long as there is prompting, direction, and specific input that move students toward accepting the "sage on the stage" role for themselves. School librarians and classroom teachers must themselves be open to research, curious about results, eager for answers, proud of self-direction, and willing to collaborate with students.

Most educators realize students have different learning styles and patterns of thought but continue the assumption that students are inherently more computer-, technology-, and web-savvy than student end-products typify. They ignore a holistic view of students' experiences that include physical dimensions of information seeking (ways of acting), cognition (ways of thinking) and affective factors (ways of feeling) (Martzoucou, 2004). When classroom teachers and school librarians overtly acknowledge the dynamics of student actions, thoughts, and emotions, they teach students how to moderate, manage, and focus the information seeking process.

Understanding the dynamics requires an involvement with students that some educators would prefer not to initiate. Because students know research is not easy, they approach it with built-in reservations and look to classroom teachers and school librarians to set the tone for how they will undertake the process. Students' observations of their teachers' behaviors impact positively or negatively how they develop their information seeking skills and use those skills for academic growth, critical thinking, and self-efficacy. Instead of acting, thinking, and feeling the assignment is too hard, students learn effective coping strategies and sound research skills for successfully completing the unit of study. End-of-unit closure consolidates behavioral, cognitive, and affective maturation. Such reflection for future inquiry-based learning offers insight and direction to classroom teachers, school librarians, and students.

Chapter 6

Research Models

Research Models and National Standards

According to *Information Power*, research models "provide students . . . with strategies for . . . finding, judging, and using information . . . that they can use both within and beyond . . . educational settings" (American Association of School Librarians & Association for Educational Communication and Technology, 1998, p. 84).

Standards for the 21st Century Learner stipulates that students "follow an inquiry-based process" (AASL, 2007).

International Society for Technology in Education's *National Educational Technology Standards—Students* (ISTE NETS-S, 2007) necessitates that students "plan strategies to guide inquiry [and] use critical thinking skills to plan and conduct research, manage projects, solve problems, and make informed decisions using appropriate digital tools and resources."

Indispensible to inquiry-based learning, research models, known as information seeking processes and problem-solving strategies, teach students information literacy skills. They combine information literacy skills needed to access and use information with information problem-solving skills. Instructional best practice requires school librarians to collaborate with classroom teachers to contextualize information problem solving with curricular content (Newell, 2009).

Research models (see Table 6.1) clearly support the standards. They enable students to move beyond the typical essay or report and become authentic investigators and problem solvers. Too often, educators, believing they are offering students a chance to explore a topic, assign a report. Because the report calls for only who, what, where, and when, the exploration becomes merely copy and paste, whether print or digital. Loertscher, Koechlin, and Zwaan's *Ban Those Birds* (2005), as an analogy, views the "birds" as the dreaded report for which students do not move beyond lower-order thinking skills. Their critical thinking is thwarted by their efforts to take shortcuts and to regurgitate the material rather than make it their own through personal understanding and analysis.

Research Models as Problem-Solving Processes

Information seeking processes (research models) involve higher-order thinking skills. The models use the action vocabularies of essential questions (see Chapter 4) and Bloom's Revised Taxonomy (see Chapter 7), such as evaluate, establish, synthesize, organize, determine, wonder, test, and compute. Consistent with a constructivist approach to education in which students build meaning from new situations, information problem-solving models (research models) require students to act on rather than to receive information. Students select and transform information, build hypotheses, and make determinations based on prior learning experiences and current knowledge (Kearsley, 2010). Actively creating knowledge and new understandings, learners assimilate ideas and information as they accommodate their beliefs and cognitive structures.

In all of the models, students demonstrate new knowledge with an original project or product. The availability of multimedia presentation software allows production of persuasive presentations. Students make decisions, create solutions, and demonstrate their findings to an audience. Web 2.0, with tools such as Voicethread, blogs, wikis, Animoto, Microsoft PhotoStory, Smilebox, and Big Huge Labs, gives students a plethora of formats.

Usually when grading reports, classroom teachers ignore the problem-solving process. An effective summative evaluation considers process and product. Students' use of the research model is as important as the final production. Periodic formative assessments during the process provide feedback to students and identify areas of weakness requiring intervention. Students use more than one domain (for instance, information seeking knowledge and subject knowledge) when working on assignments. Weakness in one knowledge domain limits overall success. Poor information search skills impede acquisition of

Table 6.1 AASL Standards, ISTE Student Standards, and Research Models

AASL Excerpted from *Standards for the 21st-Century Learner* by the American Association of School Librarians, a division of the American Library Association, copyright © 2007 American Library Association. Available for download at www.ala.org/aasl/standards. Used with permission.	ISTE NETS-S *National Educational Technology Standards for Students, Second Edition*, © 2007, ISTE® (International Society for Technology in Education), www.iste.org. All rights reserved.	Big6™	Super3™	Simple Four	Organized Investigator
Standard 1: Inquire, think critically, and gain knowledge	Standard 3: Research and Information Fluency: Students apply digital tools to gather, evaluate, and use information.	1. Task Definition 2. Information Seeking Strategies 3. Location and Access	Plan • What am I supposed to do? • What will it look like when I am done? • What do I need to find out?	Plan: • What do I need to do? • What's my research question? • What information do I need? Act: • Where can I find the information? • Which sources will be most helpful?	Questions and Wonders Finds and Sorts Consumes and Absorbs

(continued)

Table 6.1 (Continued)

AASL	ISTE NETS-S	Big6™	Super3™	Simple Four	Organized Investigator
Excerpted from *Standards for the 21st-Century Learner* by the American Association of School Librarians, a division of the American Library Association, copyright © 2007 American Library Association. Available for download at www.ala.org/aasl/standards. Used with permission.	*National Educational Technology Standards for Students*, Second Edition, © 2007, ISTE® (International Society for Technology in Education), www.iste.org. All rights reserved.				
Standard 2: Draw conclusions, make informed decisions, apply knowledge to new situations, and create new knowledge.	Standard 1: Creativity and Innovation: Students demonstrate creative thinking, construct knowledge, and develop innovative products and processes using technology.	4. Information Use 5. Synthesis: Organize information	Do • Read • View • Write • Draw a picture • Create a project	Act: • How do I decide what information I need? • Now that I've found information, what do I do with it?	Thinks and Creates Summarizes and Concludes

Communicates	Organize:	Review		Standard 2:	Standard 3:
Reflects on Process and Product	• How can I put my information together to show that I answered my question? • How can I show what I learned? • How do I document my information sources? • How can I present the information?	• Am I done? • Did I do a good job? • Do I need to change anything? • Am I happy with what I've done?	6. Synthesis: Present information 7. Evaluation	Communication and Collaboration: Students use digital media and environments to communicate and work collaboratively.	Share knowledge and participate ethically and productively as members of our democratic society.

curricular content and comprehension. Rubrics, crucial to critical thinking skill development, should include the specific steps of the adopted research model as well as desired outcomes.

Overview of Research Models

Educators have a wide array of research models from which to choose. Callison and Lamb (2009) identify 20 different models; Callison (n.d.) reviews seven of these in his book *Key Words, Concepts and Methods for Information Age Inquiry*. In addition, he covers 10 models not previously listed. All involve developing a question, identifying good sources of information, using information to create new knowledge shared with a community, and thinking about the process.

Newell (2009) identifies seven elements common to sound information seeking processes (research models):

- Task identification involves recognizing the existence of a problem.

- Search strategy initiation refers to developing a plan.

- During information location, students consider potential sources of information (books, periodicals, websites, people, databases) and identify specific resources.

- Students engage in information evaluation to determine accuracy, authority, authenticity, relevance, and usefulness.

- Information use entails integrating and synthesizing information to solve a specific problem.

- In information communication, students present their solutions to the problem.

- The final task is problem solving product/process evaluation: students reflect on both the outcome or product and the entire problem-solving process (see Table 6.2).

Although all of the models are fairly similar, some important distinctions may influence choice. Most models appear linear: a series of steps through which students progress in logical order, beginning with questions and ending with reflection or self-evaluation. Circular models appear less linear in nature. Reflection occurs at each step or follows a series of steps. Students repeat or adjust the process as the question is refined, new questions emerge, new sources are identified, or conclusions evolve. Some would argue that linear does not accurately describe their models. For example, Kuhlthau (2007) prefers to describe her seven-step ISP as sequential rather than linear because of planning for following stages and reflection on previous stages. Nevertheless, students using models often labeled linear may not engage automatically in planning or reflection unless specifically instructed. Circular models explicitly include opportunities for both.

Many of the models are long, involving six or more steps:

- Stripling and Pitts's Research Process, 10 steps

Table 6.2 Newell's Seven Information Problem-Solving Tasks and Research Models

Tasks	The Big6	The Super3	The Simple Four	Organized Investigator
Task Identification	Task Definition a. Define the problem b. Identify information requirements	Plan • What am I supposed to do? • What will it look like when I am done? • What do I need to find out?	Plan • What do I need to do? • What's my assignment? • What's my research topic? • What information do I need?	Questions and Wonders
Search Strategy Initiation	Information Seeking Strategies a. Determine range of sources b. Prioritize sources			Finds and Sorts Consumes and Absorbs
Information Location	Location and Access a. Locate sources b. Find information	Do • Read • View • Write	Act • Where can I find the information I need? • Which information sources will be most helpful?	
Information Evaluation	Information Use a. Engage with information (read, view, listen) b. Extract information	• Draw a picture • Create a project	• What search strategy will work best for each source? • Now that I've found some information what do I do with it? • How do I decide what I need from everything I've found?	Thinks and Creates

(continued)

Table 6.2 (Continued)

Tasks	The Big6	The Super3	The Simple Four	Organized Investigator
Information Use	Synthesis a. Organize the information		Organize • How can I put my information together to show that I answered my question? • How can I show what I learned? • How do I document all the information sources I used?	Summarizes and concludes
Information Communication	Synthesis b. Present the information			Communicates
Problem-Solving Product/Process Evaluation	Evaluation a. Judge the product b. Judge the process	Review • Am I done? • Did I do a good job? • Do I need to change anything? • Am I happy with what I've done?	Reflect • How will I know if I answered my question? • How will I know if I did my job well?	Reflects on process and product

Source: Newell (2009).

- Pappas and Tepe's Pathways to Knowledge, six steps
- The Big6 (Eisenberg & Berkowitz, 1987), with two sub-stages for each of the six stages, is lengthy.

Classroom teachers and school librarians should consider their students' ages and grade levels when choosing a research model. Younger students have difficulty using longer models as do older students who lack basic skills or experience. A developmental approach dictates use of simpler models in early grades to lay a foundation for more sophisticated methods later. The Super3 (Eisenberg & Berkowitz), a derivative of the Big6, uses dinosaurs, games, and songs to introduce research skills in pre-K through second grade. Upper-elementary children transition to the Big6 and employ more advanced forms by high school. The Simple Four's (School Library Media Services, South Carolina Department of Education, 2009) developmental design specifies the introduction, review, and independent use of research skills for K–12. Without assessing students' chronological and cognitive needs, school librarians who randomly apply various information seeking strategies (research models) fail to inculcate processes and skills applied across the curriculum, setting, or situation.

In districts desirous of implementing one information problem-solving model, school librarians, classroom teachers, and administrators team up to research and review various models. They compare and contrast their features and traits and choose one that best meets district needs or create their own model synthesized from the best features of each. The Baltimore Information Seeking Behavior Model is one such example (Baltimore County Public Schools, 2005). South Carolina public schools demonstrate statewide implementation with the Simple Four (Alewine, 2006). Most importantly, whatever model, once learned, is transferable. Students can apply a model to any information or research problem across curriculums and along educational continuums.

Specific Research Model Adoption

Adoption of a specific research model by a school, district, or state might increase students' facility, enhance critical thinking skills, and enable independent, lifelong learning. In some arenas, educators debate the soundness of one model versus multiple models. Although one information seeking process may offer more stability and greater chance of use as an independent life learner, some contend, by high school, students should choose the information seeking strategies that suit their cognition and desired goals.

Adoption of a research model mandates professional development. School librarians and classroom teachers need to learn the model's features as they relate to specific subject areas and curriculum. Referring to their own Pathways model, Pappas and Tepe state that school librarians should use the research model in order to instruct others on its effective application (Zimmerman, 2002). Regardless of the preferred research model, such as one of the following, multiple hours of training are essential.

Big6™

Probably the best-known, most widely used, and most commercial information problem-solving model, Big6 is both descriptive and prescriptive. Eisenberg (2001) maintains that people use Big6 steps, whether they realize it or not, whenever they solve information problems or make decisions. Big6 makes the process overt and teaches students a problem-solving strategy useful for assignments, decisions, or tasks across any life setting: school, home, and work. Best when integrated with classroom curriculum and activities, Big6 is itself a program of study with texts, workbooks, handouts, graphic organizers, lessons, and classroom aids. Workshops and webinars are offered periodically. A revised *Information, Communications and Technology Curriculum* (Eisenberg, Johnson, & Berkowitz, 2010) combines Big6 skills with ISTE's *National Educational Technology Standards for Students* (2007) to integrate fully technology and information literacy into the K–12 curriculum with the goal of student proficiency by graduation.

Super3™

Super3 is a version of Big6 skills for young students, pre-K through second grade (Eisenberg & Berkowitz, 1987). The six steps are reduced to three: Plan, Do, and Review. Each encompasses two steps from Big6 and prompts children with questions. Like its older sibling, Super3 is designed to teach information problem solving and has a wealth of material available on the web, including songs, games, handouts, and demonstration projects.

The Simple Four

Many South Carolina primary and secondary schools use the Simple Four. With four steps—plan, act, organize, and reflect—the Simple Four consists of questions students ask themselves as they proceed through the research process. These questions prompt students as they consider their research topics, information search, presentation or product, and success of work. The Simple Four website provides tools for classroom teachers, school librarians, and students. The *K–12 ICT Scope and Sequence* (School Library Media Services South Carolina Department of Education, 2009) aligns the Simple Four with AASL *Standards for the 21st Century Learner* (2007) and ISTE *National Educational Standards for Students* (2007). Applied across the curriculum, the Simple Four identifies the grades at which specific skills should be introduced, reviewed, and used independently. A *Skills Guide* (South Carolina Department of Education, 2006) compares the Simple Four with Big6 and lists related technology skills. A number of cross-curricular, technology-rich, final projects for K–12 students are suggested.

Organized Investigator (Circular Model)

David Loertscher's and Blanche Woolls's (2002) Organized Investigator breaks down into discreet stages:

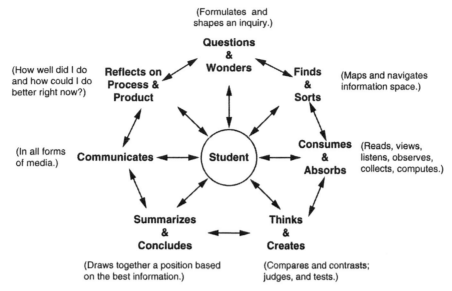

Figure 6.1 Loertscher's and Woolls's Organized Investigator. Reprinted with permission.

- Questions and Wonders

- Finds and Sorts

- Consumes and Absorbs

- Thinks and Creates

- Summarizes and Concludes

- Communicates

- Reflects on Process and Product

Placing at the center students experiencing each stage at any time and in any order, the model is depicted as a wagon wheel (see Figure 6.1). Although students may move through the stages sequentially, they should move backwards, forwards, or between stages as their focus and needs change. The terminology in the diagram implies nonlinear usage. For example, as students absorb, questions arise. The questions require additional navigation, through various information spaces, that leads to summarization or multimodal communication.

Research Models: A Metacognitive Scaffold

A search of professional and academic literature reveals little on the Simple Four and Organized Investigator. The Big6 has substantial support in the professional literature and on its website. Most of this support is anecdotal evidence, while empirical studies are rare (Wolf, Brush, & Saye, 2003). Although results obtained from these studies may not hold true for all information seeking strategies, some conclusions may be extrapolated.

For instance, Wolf and her colleagues examined Big6 as a support structure for students working just beyond their abilities. They concluded that Big6 acts as a metacognitive scaffold that (a) supports students while they learn to monitor their own thought processes, (b) provides a functional vocabulary that students and teachers use to communicate about problem-solving strategies, and (c) imparts a systematic method that students employ in other learning situations. Insofar as the Simple Four and Organized Investigator are similar to Big6, they might be considered metacognitive scaffolds.

Whether scaffolding is internalized likely depends on a number of variables, including the specific research model, type of learning environment, task assigned, and interactions between and among classroom teachers, school librarians, and students. Nevertheless, research models provide students with a framework to guide their information inquiry as they demonstrate new learning through final products.

Chapter 7

Assessments

Needs Assessment

Successful collaborative units begin with understanding students and classroom cultures. School librarians rely on classroom teachers for background about cognitive styles and abilities, interests, critical thinking and technological skills, and classroom composition, both the physical arrangement and student demographics. Such insights enable school librarians and classroom teachers to craft a unit that supports student learning, provides equitable access to all students, and fosters positive dispositions toward future independent inquiry. Students vary widely not only in their intellectual abilities, but also in their preferred learning modalities, levels of critical thinking, and information literacies: media, digital, and reading. Some may be gifted while others may have specific learning disabilities. In this mobile, diverse society, understanding diverse needs includes English for Students of Other Language (ESOL). Often reticent to seek help because they lack language confidence, students for whom English is a second language require assistive support and alternative resources.

The thorough needs assessment addresses each of the following questions:

- What learning styles do the students exhibit?
- What is the classroom's physical arrangement?

- What are the classroom demographics (racial, cultural, socioeconomic levels)?

- What are the students' digital competencies?

- What are the students' levels of reading and comprehension?

- Where are the students on Bloom's Taxonomy (LOTS or HOTS)? (Bloom, Eglehart, Furst, Hill, & Krathwohl, 1956).

- What multiple intelligences are represented? (Gardner, 1983, 1993).

- Have any of the students undergone testing for learning problems or giftedness?

- Can you justify the relevance and appropriateness of the unit in relation to students' needs?

- Do the students have access to computers and the Internet, both at home and school?

School librarians and classroom teachers want all students to have materials, resources, and technologies conducive to 21st-century learning regardless of students' ages, educational levels, ethnicities, languages, incomes, physical challenges, and geographic separations. They strive to offer equitable access within an educational system sometimes strapped by economic hardships. Often, the school setting neither supports assistive technologies for the learning disabled nor provides computers for home use. Classroom teachers and school librarians become aware of these barriers during the needs assessment and structure the unit so that all students have access to all lesson materials.

Materials presented in multiple formats (written, visual, and audio) reach the students' varying ability levels, and the final product must include alternative avenues for demonstrating new knowledge. If the assignment requires the use of electronic media and/or computers, school librarians and classroom teachers must be sure the school has adequate facilities and must schedule sufficient time.

Having electronic media and computers at their disposal does not mean that students have the technological skills presumed by both students and educators. Because students can spend hours surfing the web, playing Internet games, and manipulating the hardware, they approach scholarly assignments involving valid research with bravado. Classroom teachers and school librarians fall prey to this casualness. The presumption that "digital natives" have digital fluency leads educators to make assignments outside the students' capabilities. The popular media's label of digital natives for 21st-century children does not equate with their technological skill, cognitive ability, and emotional development. Emotions, attitudes, and motivations determine students' dispositions.

Dispositions are "ongoing beliefs and attitudes that guide thinking and intellectual behavior that can be measured by actions taken" (AASL, 2007). For instance, students may demonstrate initiative by using their own time to explore an issue or curiosity by pursuing their own interests. They may demonstrate creativity by developing innovative presentations or openness to new ideas by listening to the opinions of others. Thus, an assignment that is too difficult or too easy may discourage the development of a positive disposition. An assignment that does not connect with students' preferred modalities for learning fails to challenge critical thinking skills. Assigning too high a level of reading comprehension may result in frustration, boredom, or failure. Students experiencing these negative emotions are less likely to demonstrate behaviors consistent with a positive attitude toward learning and are less likely to engage in "learning4 life" (AASL, 2007). Often that which makes children unique holds the key to how they learn best. Consequently, a thorough and complete understanding of students' needs and abilities is imperative for the development of an engaging and successful unit.

Multiple Intelligences

Howard Gardner (1983, 1993) was an early proponent of assessing students' individual needs and designing lesson plans with multiple entry points so that all students gain access to information and demonstrate learning. His theory of multiple intelligences posited seven different intelligences (he later added an eighth), which all people possess to some extent, differing in degree and combination (see Table 7.1). Although Gardner (2006) has considered other intelligences, such as humor and moral, they do not meet his conservative criteria. He has not entirely ruled out the possibility of a ninth intelligence: existential.

Gardner (1983, 1993) believes that the focus in schools and in society on linguistic and logical-mathematic intelligences shortchanges those whose other intelligences (i.e., musical, or bodily-kinesthetic) are more highly developed. Ideally, an appropriate curriculum matches students' intelligence profile, interests, and goals. Barring that, Gardner (1993) points out that skilled teachers offer multiple routes to understanding and for demonstrating mastery. All students benefit, not just by having an entry point specific to their intelligence profile, but by experiencing cognitive flexibility, developing multiple representations of the same concept, and understanding that there are other ways of knowing.

Two decades ago, Gardner (1983, 1993), believing that interactive technologies would help to match students with the ways they learn best, predicted the educational potential of technology. He recognized that motivation would be the most significant factor in determining success of an educational program. When teachers address students' multiple intelligences, students become more confident, competent, and engaged. Technology engages students and motivates them to succeed in a domain that is highly valued by society.

Identifying students' varying intelligences relies primarily on classroom observation and students' self-report. Describing the associated skills, aptitudes, and interests, Armstrong (2003), in a book written for middle-school children, devotes a chapter to each of the eight intelligences. Classroom teachers and school librarians can adapt Armstrong's assessments that help children determine their preferred intelligence (see Table 7.2).

Critics of Gardner's theory say many of the intelligences are learning styles, talents, or abilities because they do not really constitute intelligence (Boyles & Contadino, 1997). Gardner (1983), while maintaining that his theory is unique, acknowledges that there may be some overlap and suggests that he may be trying to describe some of the same

Table 7.1 Multiple Intelligences

Intelligence	Characteristics
Linguistic	• Skilled manipulators of language; have good vocabulary and spell well • Enjoy word play • Communicate well • Enjoy reading and writing; may be good story tellers • Good at memorizing verbal and written information • Hearing, seeing, and repeating information most effective way of learning • Enjoy talking with others about ideas • May monopolize classroom conversations
Logical-Mathematical (Scientific)	• Tend to question the world around them • Inquisitive, need to find answers • Enjoy exploring patterns and relationships • Like to work with numbers • Excel at math, reasoning, logic, problem solving • Enjoy hands-on experimentation
Spatial	• Able to form mental models of world around them • Able to operate using a model • Excellent sense of direction • Enjoy looking at pictures and movies • Enjoy puzzles, mazes, maps, charts • Like to draw, build, design, and create things from memory
Musical	• Love rhythm and enjoy music • Enjoy learning to play instruments • Respond to rhythm and music with whole body • Enjoy singing • Remember melodies and tunes easily • Hum or sing while doing tasks • Like making musical sounds with body (clapping, snapping, tapping)
Bodily-Kinesthetic	• Solve problems using one's whole body • Use touch and movement to process information • Highly developed gross motor skills • Excel in physical activities: dance, sports, crafts • High energy levels: like to move around and be active • Highly coordinated • Move while thinking • Enjoy acting in skits and plays

Table 7.1 (Continued)

Interpersonal	• Good at understanding people and feelings • Good leaders: organize, motivate and communicate well with others • Learning enhanced in group situations • Enjoy group activities and discussions • Meet new people confidently • Extraverted; socializes; make friends easily • Offer to help others
Intrapersonal	• Excellent self-awareness and understanding • Introspective • Prefer to work alone rather than with others • Like to set and meet own goals • Stand-up for beliefs, even when they are not popular • Not concerned about what others think • Enjoy keeping a diary or writing in a journal • Enjoy individual assignments
Naturalist	• Enjoy being in nature • Able to identify plants and animals • Good at ordering, classifying, and categorizing • Enjoy outdoor activities (hiking, camping, fishing) • Like animals • Have a green thumb • Adapt well to different places • Like going to places like zoos, aquariums, and parks

Sources: Armstong (2003); Gardner (1983, 1993).

dimensions as those who describe styles. Regardless, Gardner's theory underscores that children receive, understand, use, and remember information in distinctive ways. Every teacher grapples with numerous, complex learning styles.

Learning Styles

All students have a preferred or characteristic way of learning, called a learning style, which is evident in the way they perceive and process information. In his Experiential Learning Theory, David Kolb proposes four modes of learning: Concrete Experience (CE), Abstract Conceptualization (AC), Active Experimentation (AE), and Reflective Observation (RO). Heredity, past experiences, and the demands of the present environment determine a person's preferred learning mode (Kolb, Boyatzis, & Mainemeles, 1999). Table 7.3 summarizes the instructional activities associated with each learning mode.

CE (concrete experience) and AC (abstract conceptualization) are opposites in terms of how people perceive or grasp information. AE (active experimentation) and RO (reflective

Table 7.2 Sample Assessment Questions

Do you:

love to read?	spell well?	enjoy playing word games?
find numbers fascinating?	easily do math in your head?	like solving mysteries?
enjoy strategy games like chess and checkers?	remember faces better than names?	like taking things apart and putting them back together?
enjoy drawing and doodling?	like to move around and be active?	dance gracefully?
excel at sports?	have street smarts?	like to people watch?
enjoy group activities?	feel confident when meeting new people?	enjoy keeping a diary?
have a green thumb?	like animals?	enjoy singing?
stand up for your beliefs even when no one agrees with you?	pay attention to your environment wherever you are?	easily pick up rhythm?

Source: Armstong (2003).

observation) form a polarity for processing or transforming information into knowledge. The intersection of these two polarities creates four distinct learning styles (Kolb, Boyatzis, & Mainemeles, 1999) (see Figure 7.1).

- *Divergers* grasp information through concrete experiences and transform these experiences into knowledge through thoughtful observation. They are good at looking at

Table 7.3 Instructional Activities for Learning Modes

Learning Mode		Instructional Activities
Perception	Concrete Experiential (learning through experience)	Small group instruction, specific examples, practical exercises, simulations, games, personal stories, role playing
	Abstract Conceptualization (learning through analysis)	Lectures, papers, analysis, model building, theorizing, questioning
Process	Active Experimentation (learning by doing)	Case studies, field work, projects, homework, hands-on activities, experiments
	Reflective Observation (learning by reflecting)	Creative problem solving, personal journals, discussion groups, brainstorming, observations, reflective papers, thought-provoking questions

Sources: Burris, Kitchel, Molina, Vincent, & Warner (2008); Sutliff & Baldwin (2001).

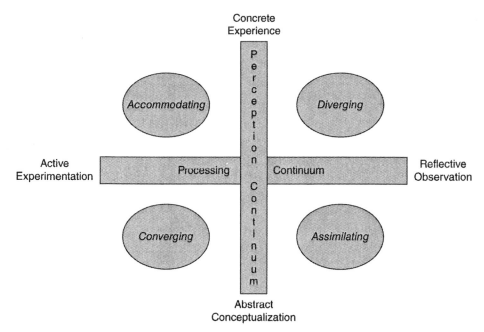

Figure 7.1 Kolb's Learning Styles. *Source*: Copyright 2007, Experienced Based Learning Systems, Inc.

situations from multiple perspectives and at generating new ideas. They enjoy gathering information, have broad cultural interests, and tend to be imaginative. They enjoy working with others.

- *Assimilators* tend to be less interested in people and more interested in ideas and abstract concepts. They understand a wide range of information when it is put into a concise, logical form. Consequently, they prefer readings, lectures, analogies, and theoretical models. They are good at inductive reasoning.

- *Convergers*, who perceive information in more abstract forms and transform it into knowledge by experimenting with it, use deductive reasoning to solve problems. They enjoy technical tasks and like to work alone. In educational settings, they prefer experiments, simulations, laboratory work, and practical application of ideas and theories.

- *Accommodators* process information through experimentation, but their experience is more concrete. They learn best from hands-on experience. Risk takers, they enjoy action-oriented group projects in which they can set and accomplish goals. They rely heavily on others for information and tend to act on intuition rather than reason (Burris, Kitchel, Molina, Vincent, & Warner, 2008; Kolb, Boyatzis, & Mainemeles, 1999). While classroom teachers and school librarians may not determine each student's learning style, they need to incorporate classroom activities and instructional strategies that address the variety of styles represented within one classroom.

Bloom's Taxonomy: Critical Thinking Skills

Just as classroom teachers and school librarians assess students' multiple intelligences and learning styles, they assess students' cognitive abilities, known as critical thinking skills.

Although originally designed for social scientists and public policy mavens as a common language for classifying educational objectives, Bloom's Taxonomy was quickly adopted by educators as a way to understand students' cognitive abilities (Bloom, Eglehart, Furst, Hill, & Krathwohl, 1956). The Taxonomy gives classroom teachers and school librarians a visual representation of children's critical thinking development on a continuum from lower to higher. Using the hierarchy, teachers identify students' current levels of functioning and set goals for progress.

In a literature lesson presenting the elements of plot (knowledge), the teacher may ask the students to *identify* the parts of the plot in a book they have read (application) and *compare* this plot to another story (analysis). Identify and compare are student actions; knowledge, application, and analysis are levels of cognition. In contrast, asking students to compare plots of two stories (analysis) without first covering elements of plot (knowledge) inhibits the student's learning progress. The teacher has lost sight of Bloom's Taxonomy with its cognitive continuum.

Bloom's Taxonomy has undergone revision in the 50 years since it was first introduced. Anderson and Krathwohl (2001) developed new terminology for each level of thought, reversed the order of Evaluation and Synthesis, and replaced Synthesis with Creating. Replacing the nouns with action words emphasizes student involvement in the learning process. The action words are verb forms, and verbs imply doing. Students relate to and carry out concrete actions (see Figure 7.2, Figure 7.3, and Table 7.4).

Multiple Literacies

Good lesson plans incorporating multiple intelligences, learning styles, and critical thinking skills ineffectively support student achievement unless they address information

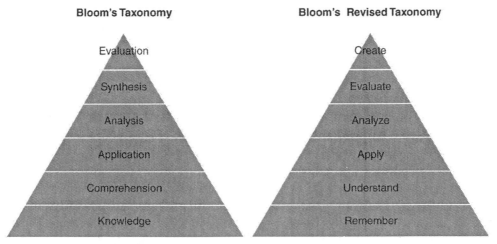

Figure 7.2 Bloom's Taxonomy. *Source*: Anderson & Krathwohl, *A taxonomy for learning, teaching, and assessing* (2001, p. 310). Copyright © 2001 Addison Wesley Longman, Inc. Reproduced by permission of Pearson Education, Inc.

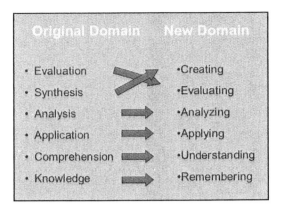

Figure 7.3 Paralleling the Taxonomy Domains. *Source*: Clark (2009).

literacies: media, digital, and reading. Media-literate students compose, comprehend, interpret, analyze, and appreciate the language and texts of both print and nonprint. Print media include books, magazines, and newspapers. Nonprint media include photography, podcasts, radio, weblogs, websites, e-books, CDs, DVDs, social networking, film, television, gaming, computer software, and virtual reality. In the 21st century, the digital format (computers, online, Internet, and virtual reality) controls nonprint media. Therefore, students must be conversant with computer technologies. Keyboarding proficiency, not addressed by some classroom teachers and school librarians, scaffolds more advanced technological skills:

- Reading an URL
- Locating and using information knowledgably
- Researching with direction and purpose
- Manipulating hardware tools
- Choosing and creating with Web 2.0
- Participating in online global communities
- Practicing responsible and ethical use of information
- Internet safety

Reading Literacy

Media and digital literacies, multiple intelligences, learning styles, and critical thinking skills hinge on reading comprehension; reading is fundamental. The design of curricula must cover students' reading and comprehension levels. Such information is readily available to classroom teachers from state-required standardized test scores. Creating a unit with multiple entry points for different levels of readers addresses both the need for equitable access and the importance of cultivating a disposition for lifelong learning. Based on testing and individual education plans, lesson designs recognize learning differences of challenged, gifted, and ESOL students. School librarians identify resources, appropriate materials, and

Table 7.4 Bloom's Taxonomy and Revision

Complexity of Thought	Bloom's Taxonomy	Anderson and Krathwohl's Revision	Actions
Higher-Order Thinking Skills (HOTS)	Evaluation	Create: the same as Bloom's Synthesis	Composing, constructing, creating, designing, developing, integrating, inventing, performing, producing
	Synthesis	Evaluate: the same as Bloom's Evaluation	Appraising, arguing, assessing, choosing, concluding, judging, justifying, proving
	Analysis	Analyze	Analyzing, diagramming, characterizing, classifying, comparing, contrasting, debating, deducing, relating, organizing
	Application	Apply	Applying, changing, choosing, computing, dramatizing, preparing, selecting, showing, using
	Comprehension	Understand	Comprehending, explaining, discussing, illustrating, paraphrasing, predicting, summarizing
Lower-Order Thinking Skills (LOTS)	Knowledge	Remember	Knowing, recalling, recognizing, memorizing, naming, reciting, counting, identifying, describing

Source: Anderson & Krathwohl (2001, p. 310).

alternative formats with similar information presented at varying levels of ability. For instance, students who have reading disabilities may use assistive technologies, books-on-tape, or Playaways. Gifted students may require materials above their grade level. Regardless of ability level, students can exceed their own and others' expectations when motivated by interesting units of study; nevertheless, the learning environment can make or break any unit.

Classroom Culture

Classroom teachers and school librarians should consider classroom culture and arrangement. Factors such as ethnicity, race, culture, and socioeconomic level can impact classroom culture, student motivation and participation, and parental support for learning.

The room's physical layout and décor create a sense of place, where students feel supported, interact comfortably, and cultivate multicultural awareness.

Cognitive styles and abilities, interests, levels of critical thinking, technological skills, and classroom composition, both the physical arrangement and student demographics, make up the components of the students' needs assessment. Without as much of this information as possible, school librarians are handicapped in their efforts to work collaboratively with classroom teachers to bring about a more enriched student learning environment.

Formative Assessment

Not always can educators handle assessment collaboratively, but when that is the case, there is more objectivity because "two heads are better than one." Classroom teachers and school librarians temper one another's response to an activity or strategy and how to handle it in regard to the unit of study as a whole. While devising the ongoing assessments for the study unit, classroom teachers and school librarians more effectively communicate and create assessments of higher quality. Even though they regret the time consumed by such efforts, the results embody stronger pedagogical practice. When working alone, teachers will use time as the factor deterring them from working to give students more frequent and more definitive formative assessments. As a team, classroom teachers and school librarians realize their collaborative time affords students better and more instructionally strong assessments.

Goal of Formative Assessment

What is the major goal of formative assessment? Some would say that it shows students on a regular basis whether they are attaining the knowledge required for state standardized tests used to measure school accountability. They would stop with that definition; nevertheless, students hope for more. Students want to see how they measure up individually—skills, cognition, dispositions, and responsibility. Personal assessment is much more than preparation for yearly testing; learning to learn is vital for life in the 21st century.

Thus, it seems, formative assessment should weave the learner into success measurements used throughout units of study. Today's educational environment puts "self-" before such words as efficacy, enrichment, responsibility, and esteem to indicate one's empowerment in one's learning.

> Allowing students a "place at the table" when establishing the unit's goals and objectives gives students ownership.

That does not make formative assessment easier, since now classroom teachers and school librarians must take into account student behaviors and attitudes (dispositions) that will influence assessment tools. Although students have had input into assessments used, one cannot make the assumption they will be fully motivated to carry out the goals and objectives to the best of their abilities.

Motivation is constant and ongoing, and it is entwined in the fabric of learning and assessment strategies. Motivation begins with a common vision. Classroom teachers and school librarians working together envision goals for the unit of study. They design activities and strategies based on goals, and they offer insights for students' successful engagement. Students have maps in the form of rubrics for wending their way to the goals. Along the way, there are supporting evaluations. These evaluations, known as formative assessments, are not there to discourage or derail student efforts but rather to give renewed encouragement and to shore up areas not yet fully grasped or comprehended.

Formative assessment determines whether a concept needs reteaching or additional demonstration; formative assessment indicates either a change in instruction or a change in student behavior concerning the task. Change for whatever reason is more often than not resisted because even if a present pattern of response or behavior creates negative results, those faced with change rationalize, make excuses, or feign acceptance. Formative assessment must motivate by building confidence. When student achievement improves, school improvement manifests itself through higher standardized test scores, an overarching goal of today's educational institutions.

Development of "Self": Dispositions, Attitudes, and Behaviors

Those who experience success on assessments gain a strong sense of academic self-efficacy. Those who experience failure lose their sense of control over their own academic well-being (Stiggins, 2009). Students' dispositions toward subject matter and strategies for teaching and learning directly affect their skills and cognition. Learning opportunities that engage students' thinking must measure levels of success. Formative assessments used throughout a unit of study, if encouraging and corrective without being punitive, shape attitudes that in turn impinge on cognition and skill development. Classroom teachers' yearly record keeping as a chart of student growth indicates where students faltered; what strategies worked; and, through reflection and student feedback, why some techniques succeeded and others failed.

Good formative assessments have intrinsic value: students gain self-enrichment and self-esteem. Formative assessments motivate students to demonstrate learning. They foster pride in skill development, enjoyment in academic growth, and positive attitudes toward subject knowledge. Students understand their roles in the teaching/learning process; their participation in formative structures empowers them. One framework for exploring motivational strategies is Keller's ARCS (Attention, Relevance, Confidence, Satisfaction) Model of Motivational Design (as cited in Thomas, 2004).

- *Attention*: Classroom teachers and school librarians stimulate interest and curiosity. One successful technique is the KWHL: what do I know, what do I want to know, how will I find answers, and what have I learned? By reviewing prior knowledge (what do I know), classroom teachers and school librarians assure students they have a foundation for success with the new material (what do I want to know). They have the students' attention for seeking answers (how will I find answers), and summative assessments require constructivist application (what have I learned).

- *Relevance*: Many students feel they will never need what they are supposed to learn. They become indifferent, lackadaisical, or difficult until they can see value, whether utilitarian, monetary, or personal. If classroom teachers and school librarians answer the question "How will I ever use (or need) this?" with practical and/or intrinsic applications, they establish relevance. That relevance motivates students toward the unit's goal.

- *Confidence*: Students' self-confidence develops from self-awareness of one's place within the learning process. Students' confidence grows by having pertinent and positive formative assessments throughout the unit of study.

- *Satisfaction*: Expectation of success creates satisfaction. Aware of students' potential, classroom teachers and school librarians devise formative assessments that actualize potential for success. Progress on successive assessments builds students' confidence toward accomplishment of the unit's goals. The "self-" words, if the unit succeeds, empower the students: self-efficacy, self-esteem, self-worth, and self-fulfillment.

Examples of Formative Assessment

Designing formative assessments that take into account learning styles, multiple intelligences, and differences and similarities supports attention, relevance, confidence and satisfaction. Formative assessments that encourage ARCS are daily journal entries; exit Q&A; shared wiki; instructional games, either Smartboard, online, or paper/pencil; student-designed trading cards; blogging; classroom teachers', school librarians', and students' observations (not particularly useful unless followed by one-on-one communication); reading aloud; graphic organizers; note-taking matrix; skits; thumbs up–thumbs down strategy; Venn diagrams; pair-share; review of rubric levels of proficiency; end-of-class verbal sharing; and Post-It questions submitted anonymously to classroom teachers.

The examples suggest interaction, affirmation, active involvement, communication, and assurance. Formative assessment differs from evaluation in that it avoids judgment. No number or letter grade is ascribed. Formative assessment is unrestricted, nonlinear, and personal. It must be so if it is to allow opportunities for students to find their learning level and complete the work successfully. Evaluation is characterized by doing *to* the student, whereas assessment is doing *with* the student (Thomas, 2004). That is why classroom teachers and school librarians find observation followed by individual, brief conferences effective strategies for ARCS.

Classroom teachers and school librarians use observations and individual conferences, favorite tools for assessing student performances, effectively when attention, relevance, confidence, and satisfaction motivate them. Interaction, affirmation, active involvement, communication, and assurance create a safe and productive working relationship and characterize successful collaboration. Their sense of well-being and confidence in materials covered, methods, and processes influence their success in creating activities and strategies useful in formative assessment. Activities and strategies, either constructivist or traditional, focus on content.

> Without periodic review of their content learning, students cannot gather their understandings into a confirmable expression of new knowledge.

Formative assessment is not extraneous but essential for guiding students toward the summative assessment. Shaping learning through meaningful activities and strategies helps the students more clearly see how to synthesize and demonstrate understanding and knowledge of the covered materials. Throughout the unit of study, all formative assessments point students toward the ultimate assessment: the summative. If classroom teachers and school librarians create formative assessment occasions that enhance the students' learning, summative assessment showcases students' creativity, synthesis, and analysis—chances to confirm, in new ways, what students learned and where they will continue to grow.

Summative Assessment

The key distinction between formative and summative assessments is the purpose of the evaluation. Summative, used after instruction, measures student learning relative to some standard (usually content standards) and/or evaluates the success of instructional programs (Coffey, n.d.; Garrison & Ehringhaus, n.d.). Traditionally used to make decisions regarding student placement, effectiveness of teaching methods, school goals, alignment of curriculum to state standards, and funding, summative assessment supposedly determines what students know or do not know (Bransford, Brown, & Cocking, 1999). Often referred to as high-stakes testing due to potential consequences for students, programs, schools, and districts, summative assessment (using multiple choice, true/false, or matching) compares students' scores to a normal distribution of scores for students taking the same test. In many schools, districts, and states, interpretations based on a single test score have been used to place students in low-track classes, require them to repeat a grade, or deny a diploma. Examples of traditional summative assessments include the following:

- Statewide accountability tests

- District benchmark or interim testing

- End-of-unit or chapter tests

- End-of-term or semester exams

- Scores used for Annual Yearly Progress (AYP)

- Report card grades (Coffey, n.d.; Garrison & Ehringhaus, n.d.; Winking & Bond, 1995)

Such uses narrowly define student learning as factual knowledge and summative assessments as tests that result in scores or grades. They fail to ascertain whether students know when, where, why, and how to use their knowledge.

Performance Assessment as Authentic Assessment

A broader definition of summative assessment focuses more on students' understandings and abilities to apply new knowledge appropriately. Alternatives to tests and exams include authentic, performance, and project-based assessments that require students to construct a response, engage in a task, or create a product that demonstrates skills and knowledge (Elliot, 1995; Sweet, 1993; Winking, 1997). Although often used synonymously, authentic and performance assessments spring from distinct educational purposes (Wiggins, 1998).

- Performance assessments originate in vocational education and find additional application in practical areas such as engineering, automotive repair, and music where demonstration of proficiency is more highly correlated with success than the ability to recall facts (Palm, 2008).

- Authentic assessments are a response to dissatisfaction with norm-referenced standardized tests (Palm, 2008). Used with more academic or theoretical subjects such as mathematics or literature, authentic assessment seeks to evaluate students' abilities to assimilate and apply knowledge in useful, real-world contexts.

Practically, the distinction between performance and authentic assessment is thin; both require active problem solving, application and manipulation of knowledge, and demonstration of proficiency or mastery. By this definition, performance assessment is authentic.

Authentic Assessment Defined

"Authentic intellectual work requires the construction of knowledge, through disciplined inquiry, to produce discourse, products, or performances that have meaning beyond success in school" (Newmann, King, & Carmichael, 2007, p. 5). Knowledge construction involves the use of higher-order thinking skills (HOTS) taught through repeated activities and experiences. Disciplined inquiry, building on prior knowledge, has as its goal in-depth understanding. Students develop and share their insights, ideas, and conclusions through "elaborated communication" (Newmann, King, & Carmichael, 2007, p. 4). Although elaborated communications often take the form of essays or research papers, Newmann and his colleagues allow that they may take other complex forms using verbal, symbolic, graphic, and visual tools. The use of technology is not mentioned specifically; however, Web 2.0

applications empower students to demonstrate mastery of both process (procedures and strategies) and content (knowledge) through the creation of product or performance. Finally, to have value beyond mere success in school, the assignment must be relevant, both to the world outside the classroom and to the student personally.

Authentic assessments create a more active learning environment than traditional summative assessments. Many classroom teachers, responding to high-stakes testing, "teach to the test." Memorization and recall require little student engagement or participation. Authentic assessments enable classroom teachers to meet standards and move beyond with creativity and improved pedagogy. When classroom teachers connect learning to the real world by providing worthwhile activities, students exhibit increased learning, greater motivation, and more active involvement (Newmann, King, & Carmichael, 2007; Sweet, 1993).

Use of authentic assessment fulfills AASL's (2007) *Standards for the 21st-Century Learner* and ISTE's (2007) *National Educational Technology Standards for Students.* Both sets of standards support the definition of authentic intellectual work: the construction of knowledge through disciplined inquiry, to create projects, performances, and products that have meaning beyond success in school (Newmann, King, & Carmichael, 2007) (see Table 7.5).

Authentic Assessment and the Role of School Librarians

School librarians' involvement in authentic assessment is the key to collaboration's success. Classroom teachers focus on content standards; school librarians focus on information literacy and technology standards. School librarians expand the learning environment beyond the classroom to encompass the library media center and website, Internet, and community. Community resources include other libraries (public and academic), museums, nonprofit organizations, businesses, and individuals with expertise in curricular or unit topics. School librarians identify wide varieties of information sources and formats to meet the learning needs of all students. School librarians teach the research model (information search process), incorporate information literacy (how to find, evaluate, use, analyze, and synthesize information in all of its forms), and build students' technology skills.

School librarians suggest and develop the format for the authentic assessment. Their education and training emphasize the use of alternative information delivery systems. Examples of authentic assessment are diverse and wide ranging. Oral interviews, story or text retelling, reenactments, exhibitions, experiments, demonstrations, poster presentations, plays, artwork, journals, portfolios, newspaper articles, models, and the ubiquitous Power-Point epitomize strong authentic assessment tools. Technology facilitates multimedia productions. School librarians teach use of Web 2.0 tools for producing podcasts, videocasts, websites, wikis, mind-maps, Voicethreads, Animoto trailers, PhotoStory presentations, graphs, charts, surveys, and polls. Possibilities are limited only by educators' and students' imaginations and the school's fair-use policy.

Table 7.5 Comparison: Authentic Intellectual Work, *Standards for the 21st-Century Learner*, and *National Educational Technology Standards for Students*

Authentic Intellectual Work (Newmann, King, & Carmichael, 2007)	AASL: Excerpted from *Standards for the 21st-Century Learner* by the American Association of School Librarians, a division of the American Library Association, copyright © 2007 American Library Association. Available for download at www.ala.org/aasl/standards. Used with permission.	*National Educational Technology Standards for Students*, Second Edition, © 2007, ISTE® (International Society for Technology in Education), www.iste.org. All rights reserved.
Higher-Order Thinking Skills	**1.1.7** Make sense of information gathered from diverse sources by identifying misconceptions, main and supporting ideas, conflicting information, and point of view or bias. **1.2.4** Maintain a critical stance by questioning the validity and accuracy of all information **2.1.1** Continue an inquiry-based research process by applying critical-thinking skills (analysis, synthesis, evaluation, organization) to information and knowledge in order to construct new understandings, draw conclusions, and create new knowledge.	**3.b** Locate, organize, analyze, evaluate, synthesize, and ethically use information from a variety of sources and media. **4.** Students use critical thinking skills to plan and conduct research, manage projects, solve problems, and make informed decisions using appropriate digital tools and resources. Students: **c.** Collect and analyze data to identify solutions and/or make informed decisions. **d.** Use multiple processes and diverse perspectives to explore alternative solutions.
Depth of Knowledge	**1.1.6** Read, view, and listen for information presented in any format (e.g. textual, visual, media, digital) in order to make inferences and gather meaning. **2.2.1** Demonstrate flexibility in the use of resources by adapting information strategies to each specific resource and by seeking additional resources when clear conclusions cannot be drawn.	**1.a** Apply existing knowledge to generate new ideas, products, or processes. **1.c** Use models and simulations to explore complex systems and issues. **6.** Students demonstrate a sound understanding of technology concepts, systems, and operations. Students:

(continued)

Table 7.5 (Continued)

Authentic Intellectual Work (Newmann, King, & Carmichael, 2007)	AASL: Excerpted from *Standards for the 21st-Century Learner* by the American Association of School Librarians, a division of the American Library Association, copyright © 2007 American Library Association. Available for download at www.ala.org/aasl/standards. Used with permission.	*National Educational Technology Standards for Students*, Second Edition. © 2007, ISTE® (International Society for Technology in Education), www.iste.org. All rights reserved.
	4.2.3 Maintain openness to new ideas by considering divergent opinions, changing opinions or conclusions when evidence supports the change, and seeking new ideas encountered through academic and personal experiences.	**a.** Understand and use technology systems. **b.** Select and use applications effectively and productively. **c.** Troubleshoot systems and applications **d.** Transfer current knowledge to learning new technologies.
Connection to the World	1.1.1 Follow an inquiry-based process in seeking knowledge in curricular subjects, and make real-world connection for using this process in own life. 2.1.3 Use strategies to draw conclusions from information and apply knowledge to curricular areas, real-world situations, and further investigations. 2.3.1 Connect understanding to the real world. 2.3.2 Consider diverse and global perspective in drawing conclusions. 3.3.4 Create products that apply to authentic, real-world contexts.	**2.c** Develop cultural understanding and global awareness by engaging with learners of other cultures. **4.a** Identify and define authentic problems and significant questions for investigation.

Substantive Conversation	**1.1.9** Collaborate with others to broaden and deepen understanding. **1.3.4** Contribute to the exchange of ideas within the learning community. **2.1.5** Collaborate with others to exchange ideas, develop new understandings, make decisions, and solve problems. **3.1.2** Participate and collaborate as members of a social and intellectual network of learners. **3.2.2** Show social responsibility by participating actively with others in learning situations and by contributing questions and ideas during group discussions.	**2.** Students use digital media and environments to communicate and work collaboratively, including at a distance, to support individual learning and contribute to the learning of others. Students: **a.** Interact, collaborate, and publish with peers, experts or others employing a variety of media and formats. **b.** Communicate information and ideas effectively to multiple audiences using a variety of media and formats. **c.** Contribute to project teams to produce original works or solve problems.
Social Support for Student Achievement	**1.4.2** Use interaction with and feedback from teachers and peers to guide own inquiry process. **3.4.3** Assess own ability to work with others in a group setting be evaluating varied roles, leadership, and demonstrations of respect for other viewpoints.	**5.b** Exhibit a positive attitude toward using technology that supports collaboration, learning, and productivity. **5.c** Demonstrate personal responsibility for lifelong learning. **5.d** Exhibit leadership for digital citizenship.

Authentic assessments empower classroom teachers and school librarians to meet individual needs of students. During the needs assessment, classroom teachers and school librarians identify students with varying multiple intelligences, learning styles, abilities or disabilities, and English-language competence. Authentic assessments provide creative alternatives for students to demonstrate and apply constructed knowledge and for educators to evaluate learning. Students with kinesthetic intelligence or for whom English is a second language may choose to construct a model, while students who have interpersonal intelligence or who have the accommodator learning style may work together to initiate a school-wide program. Students with developmental disorders or learning disabilities may demonstrate new aptitudes or proficiencies using online technologies.

An Example of Inquiry-Based Learning and Authentic Assessment

A middle-school unit on states' water rights issues beautifully illustrates inquiry-based learning and authentic assessment. Using the Big6 model, students researched the recent controversy over water rights in Georgia, Alabama, and Florida. They created an electronic mind-map as they brainstormed research questions; used a wiki to take notes and share information; used websites, online databases, and portals to find and evaluate information; incorporated science, social studies, geography, and math; created an online survey, analyzed the responses and graphed the results; and developed a PowerPoint, which they presented to a local conservation organization. Formative assessment during the project provided feedback and allowed adjustments of instructional techniques. The PowerPoint presentation was the basis for authentic, summative assessment. The students, having little or no previous experience with PowerPoint, worked on an engaging, worthwhile project with real-world implications and impact; met content, information literacy, and technology standards; and applied their new knowledge and skills to create new understandings. The wide variety of tasks and educational formats presented options for students with differing learning styles and needs.

Equitable Authentic Assessment

Authentic assessments must be equitable; they must provide all students with opportunities to demonstrate learning and progress. That "[a]ll children deserve equitable access to books and reading, to information, and to information technology in an environment that is safe and conducive to learning" is a common belief identified by AASL's (2007) *Standards for the 21st-Century Learner*. Guidelines for equitable assessment often restate best practice. For instance, Winking (1997) advises that educators provide students with scaffolding activities (information search processes) to support their learning and that performance criteria be explicit and clearly understood by each student (use of rubrics). Koelsch, Estrin, and Farr (1995) suggest linking assessment to students' experiences in and out of the classroom (prior learning) and to their known ways of thinking and demonstrating learning (multiple intelligences and learning styles). They recommend that assessments promote connections between school learning and the local context (connection to the real world) and that more than one measure be used to evaluate student learning.

The following are recommendations for equitable authentic assessments:

- Link assessment content to students' experiences, perspectives, and prior knowledge.

- Construct assessments to match students' ways of thinking and learning and to access multiple ways of knowing.

- Allow accommodations for second-language learners, cultural groups, and students with disabilities.

- Be sure that performance criteria are explicit and clearly understood by each student.

- Allow students choices for assessment tasks, materials, and response modes whenever possible.

- Allow students sufficient time to experiment with and complete the assessment format or mode prior (formative assessment) to the summative assessment.

- Provide students with scaffolding activities to support new learning.

- Develop assessments that connect school knowledge with local context.

- Use more than one measure to evaluate student learning (Koelsch, Estrin, & Farr, 1995; Winking, 1997).

Traditional Assessment with Authentic Assessment

Even when teaching for in-depth understanding, some classroom teachers feel more comfortable with traditional, less authentic assessment emphasizing memorization, practice, and recall. When students and teachers utilize traditional summative evaluations, results can guide efforts and activities in subsequent units or classes. Classroom teachers and school librarians should not rule out paper-and-pencil tests because in a collaborative unit, classroom teachers and school librarians apply them in tandem with alternative, project-based assessments. Classroom teachers grade tests, and school librarians evaluate constructed knowledge. Both forms of assessment provide important information to students, parents, and educators, and together meet educational standards: content standards as well as information literacy and technology standards. By incorporating alternative summative assessments, collaboration enables students to demonstrate and apply their learning in creative formats that stretch their critical thinking skills and problem solving.

Alternative assessments boost students' engagement with learning. Assessments that capitalize on prior knowledge and involve students in designing the final product increase motivation (Winking, 1997). A clear understanding of the assignment, of what students are expected to know and do, enhances their engagement (Elliot, 1995; Sweet, 1993; Winking, 1997). Authentic assessment positively influences student performance by

- developing tasks or assignments that clearly align with content standards: Classroom teachers post standards in classrooms and/or provide them in a handout and discuss ways in which the collaborative unit will cover each standard.

- providing students with models of acceptable performance prior to the task: If students are expected to produce an Animoto trailer or a Prezi, classroom teachers and school librarians should develop their own as a demonstration and highlight how it meets project requirements. The model orients students; they can refer to it as they work on their own projects.

- sharing scoring criteria (rubrics) with students prior to the task: Up-front specification of task requirements clarifies expectations and helps students set realistic goals. Classroom teachers and school librarians carefully describe good performance in detail.

- building student self-assessment into scoring criteria: When students help to establish criteria for judging their work by themselves and by others, they are more likely to work toward goals.

Rubrics

Rubrics' primary goal is to measure students' learning, converted from information to knowledge through practiced critical thinking. Rubrics cover operationally defined behaviors and dispositions. They are rating systems for determining levels of proficiency at which students are able to perform a task or display knowledge (Brualdi, 1998). Constructed as grids or tables, rubrics list target skills or indicators (criteria) down the left side and levels of proficiency across the top. Each criterion and level of proficiency must be clearly and explicitly defined. Typically, rubrics have at least three criteria and three levels of proficiency. Criteria include mastery of subject content, cross-curricular requirements (such as good grammar and composition in a science project), and inquiry-based skills. Rubrics, crucial to information literacy development, specify steps of the adopted research model as well as desired outcomes. Students' performances on each criterion are rated. Levels of proficiency may be defined verbally (i.e., poor, meets expectations, or exceeds expectations), with graphics, points, narrative feedback, or a combination of these. The overall score or outcome contributes to the grade.

Distributed at the onset of the unit, rubrics provide students with an advanced organizer and a clear statement of requirements for success. Advantages of rubrics are many (Brualdi, 1998; Callison, n.d.):

- They increase objectivity. Classroom teachers and school librarians evaluate students against specific criteria rather than other students or their own past performance.

- They help classroom teachers and school librarians focus on essential knowledge, skills, and processes. When used formatively, they guide the instructional process.

- As part of the information seeking process (research model), rubrics give students a visual representation of their progress.

- Feedback is easy to convey and improves communication with students, parents, and other educators.

- In collaborations, rubrics improve grading reliability and validity between classroom teachers and school librarians.

Construction of a good rubric takes time and practice, particularly when defining criteria and levels of proficiency. The range of proficiency must be wide enough to show and encourage student progress. Brualdi (1998) suggests the following steps when developing rubrics:

1. Identify the authentic product or performance and create it.

2. List all essential aspects or components of the performance or product.

3. With the collaborative partner, identify the most important behaviors and components of the assignment.

4. Express criteria in terms of observable student behaviors and product characteristics.

5. Limit the number of criteria.

6. Arrange criteria in order of importance or in the order observed.

7. Use clear, precise language. Avoid ambiguous terms.

8. Involve students in the process. Ask them to identify elements of the project essential for determining success.

Usually, classroom teachers and school librarians create rubrics; however, students can make their own effort and achievement rubrics (Marzano, Pickering, & Pollock, 2001). Not only could rubrics give students opportunities for critical thinking when establishing their criteria, but also could afford creative opportunities for rating. Besides Likert scales, students might use icons or unconventional words to reflect levels of accomplishment. For example, if the project dealt with a look at various USA cultural decades, the terms used might be "groovy," "the quo," and "bummer."

Student self-assessment using rubrics allows students opportunities to reflect on their work, the learning process, and areas in need of improvement. When conducted in conversation (individual conferencing) with classroom teachers or school librarians, self-assessment affords insight into students' thought processes, assimilation and accommodation of new material, and knowledge construction.

Sample Authentic Assessment Activities and Rubrics

Instructions for Animoto on Baroque Art, Architecture, and Music

You will make an Animoto demonstrating your knowledge of the Baroque period. Answer the following questions in your Animoto:

1. When was the Baroque period?

2. What are the characteristics that define Baroque art, architecture, and music?

3. What were the major historical influences on art during this period?

4. Who were some of the major artists, architects, and composers of the Baroque period?

5. What were some of their works?

Your Animoto will include images:

- Paintings
- Sculptures
- Buildings
- Artists
- Composers
- Architects

It will also include text:

- Names of artists, architects and composers
- Dates
- Characteristics of Baroque art, architecture, and music

Choose a piece of music by a Baroque composer for your Animoto.

After you complete your Animoto, write a one-paragraph analysis of the Baroque period and a one-paragraph reflection on the project. Your analysis should answer all of the above questions. Your reflection is your opportunity to share your thoughts on the project:

- Your thoughts about Baroque art
- Your favorite artist, architect, or composer (explain your choice)
- Your favorite artwork or building (explain your choice)
- Your thoughts about using Animoto
- What you learned
- What you would do differently

Written work will be graded for grammar, spelling, punctuation, and composition, as well as content.

Create a reference page including all images used, your sources of information, and a citation for the music.

Based on the rubric for the Animoto product (see Table 7.6):

Total possible points: 60

Grading Scale:	A	51–60 pts.
	B	41–50 pts.
	C	31–40 pts.
	D	20–39 pts.
	F	Below 20 pts.

Your total: _____ Your Grade: _____

Table 7.6 Rubric for Student Product Using Animoto

Points Earned	0	1	2	3	4
Characteristics	0	1	2	3	4 or more
Artists	0	1	2	3	4 or more
Architects	0	1	2	3	4 or more
Composers	0	1	2	3	4 or more
Paintings	0	1	2	3	4 or more
Sculptures	0	1	3	3	4 or more
Buildings	0	1	2	3	4 or more
Baroque Music	No				Yes
Analysis	Not included or answers only 1 question	Answers 2 questions	Answers 3 questions	Answers 4 questions	Answers 5 or more questions
Reflection	Not included or answers only 1 questions	Answers 2 questions	Answers 3 questions	Answers 4 questions	Answers 5 or more questions

(continued)

Table 7.6 (Continued)

Points Earned	0	1	2	3	4
Grammar	4 or more errors	3 errors	2 errors	1 error	No errors
Spelling	4 or more errors	3 errors	2 errors	1 error	No errors
Punctuation	4 or more errors	3 errors	2 errors	1 error	No errors
Reference Page	Not included	• Includes few sources • 5 or 6 errors	• Includes some sources • 3 or 4 errors	• Includes most sources • 1 or 2 errors	• Includes all sources • No errors

Required Elements for Astronomy Voicethread

As you follow the requirements for your Voicethread, use the attached rubric (see Table 7.7).

1. Earth and moon

2. Sun

3. Three planets and rings/moons. Each planet must include:
   a. Size relative to earth
   b. Surface and atmosphere
   c. Distance from sun
   d. Life forms

4. Kuiper Belt or Oort Cloud

5. Asteroid Belt and asteroid

6. Map of galaxy or solar system

7. At least two of the following:
   a. Geocentric and heliocentric theories
   b. Big Bang
   c. Gravity

8. Extra content

Table 7.7 Rubric for Voicethread Assignment

	Awesome!	Right On!	Oops!
Voicethread Content (See checklist of required elements.) (classroom teacher)	• Voicethread contains all required elements and some extra content	• Voicethread contains all or most of the required elements	• Voicethread contains some of the required elements
Grammar and Punctuation (classroom teacher)	• Story Board (final draft) contains few or no errors	• Story Board (final draft) contains some errors	• Story Board (final draft) contains many errors
Citations (school librarian)	• MLA citation provided for each source with few or no errors; • Voicethread includes credit page	• MLA citations provided for most sources with some errors; • Voicethread includes credit page	• MLA citations provided for few or no sources and/or many errors; • Voicethread does not include credit page
Voicethread Technology (school librarian)	• Voicethread matches Story Board (final draft) • Voicethread demonstrates mastery of technology (e.g., includes a variety of images and incorporates voice recording, typed comments, and doodles	• Voicethread mostly follows Story Board (final draft) • Voicethread demonstrates familiarity with technology (e.g., includes a number of images and incorporates some of the tools)	• Voicethread does not follow the Story Board (final draft) • Voicethread demonstrates difficulty using the technology
Use of Pathfinder (school librarian)	• Voicethread demonstrates extensive use of resources identified on the Pathfinder	• Voicethread demonstrates some use of resources identified on the Pathfinder	• Voicethread demonstrates little or no use of resources identified on the Pathfinder
Collaborating with Others (teacher and school librarian)	• Partners worked very well together and completed the Voicethread without any problems	• Partners worked well most of the time but needed some assistance from the teacher/school librarian	• Partners did not work well together and required intervention by teacher/librarian

Instructions for John Smith Glog

You will make a Glog about John Smith using Glogster EDU. Your Glog will include the following Glogster tools: images, graphics, text, draw, and sound. Refer to the attached rubric for guidance (see Table 7.8).

Table 7.8 Rubric for John Smith Glog

	0 pts.	1 pt.	2 pts.	Score
Use of Technology	Glog uses < 4 tools.	Glog uses < 4 tools.	Glog use all five required tools.	
Glog	Glog incomplete	• Poorly designed • Crowded or too much empty space • Lacks aesthetic appeal • Not fun	• Interesting • Aesthetically pleasing • Well-organized • Fun to observe	
Images	Uses < 3 images	Uses < 5 images	Uses 5 or more images	

Biography/ Sound Recording	• Does not explain images
	• Does not include required information
		• Explains most images
		• Includes most of required information
			• Explains why all images are included in poster
			• Includes:
			  ○ Birth and death dates
			  ○ Other important dates
			  ○ Important people
			  ○ Highlights from Smith's life
			  ○ Important accomplishments
			  ○ Smith's contributions to history	

Grammar	3 or more errors	1–2 errors	0 errors	
Spelling	3 or more errors	1–2 errors	0 errors	

Table 7.8 (Continued)

	0 pts.	1 pt.	2 pts.	Score
Punctuation	3 or more errors	1–2 errors	0 errors	
Narration	Incomprehensible	Difficult to understand; monotone	Clear; good pronunciation; uses a variety of inflections	
Score				

1. Obtain images online. Obtain citation information for all images used.

2. Write a brief biography about John Smith. You will use this biography as the script for the sound recording you will embed in your Glog. You may need to write more than one draft. Obtain classroom teacher's okay before making the recording. Your biography will be related to (or somehow explain) every image included in your Glog. Information to include: birth and death dates, other important dates, important people, highlights from Captain Smith's life, important accomplishments, and his contribution to history.

3. Use of graphics should enhance the visual display in some way.

4. Use text and draw to highlight important information or to explain images on your Glog.

5. Citations page must accompany written biography. Citations must be listed in alphabetical order. You may want to create a word document to record citations as you use images. Toggle between Glog and document as you work. Please use the following formats.

   • For images:
     Artist's Last Name, first initial. (date). *Title of Work.* Retrieved Date from website name at web address.

   • For books:
     Author's last name, first initial. (date). *Title.* City of publication: Publisher.

   • For websites:
     Author's last name, first initial (if given). (Date). Name of Website. URL.

Chapter 8

Use of Reflection

From Prior Knowledge through Authentic Assessment

Reflection is part of a constructivist process in which people think carefully and deeply and connect new learning to old in order to create more complex and interrelated knowledge. It involves looking for commonalities, differences, and interrelationships (Clark, 2008). A powerful strategy for building knowledge and improving retention, reflection, done well, promotes higher-order thinking skills (HOTS)—analysis, synthesis, evaluation, and creativity (Milam, 2005). When students engage in reflection, they consider not only what they have learned, but how they have learned, and how the process has changed them. When school librarians and classroom teachers reflect, they consider the effectiveness of their teaching methods, whether the students have met the standards and demonstrate HOTS, and their ability to work together to promote student growth.

Reflection does not occur just at the end of the unit—it occurs throughout (see Table 8.1). Reflection begins when classroom teachers and school librarians ask students to consider their prior learning and experiences. Instead of jumping into learning new facts and information, students are invited to think about what they already know, how their knowledge is significant, and how it will contribute to classroom scholarship. Review of essential questions encourages students to think deeply about issues that go beyond the classroom to real-world experiences. Inquiry-based learning with students' own questions move students from passive receivers of information to active constructors of knowledge. Students evaluate their information seeking behaviors to determine what works, what does not, and why. Information search models (research models) offer opportunities for reflection with questions such as "What do I need to know?" "Where can I find information?" and "Have I accomplished my goal?" (Consider the KWHL.) Formative assessments give students opportunities to reflect on their progress and revise work, while summative assessment ties everything together, consolidates learning, and identifies paths for future discoveries.

AASL's *Standards for the 21st-Century Learner* (2007) incorporates student reflection. Each of the four standards includes self-assessment strategies—behaviors students use to monitor their own learning and progress (see Table 8.2).

ISTE's (2008) *National Educational Technology Standards for Teachers* (NETS-T) includes reflection, not specifically mentioned in the *National Educational Technology Standards for Students*. According to NETS-T, classroom teachers promote student reflection in collaborative units to encourage and reveal critical thinking skills and creativity. Teachers reflect on their professional practice and use of technology.

Table 8.1 Reflection from Prior Knowledge through Authentic Assessment

Prior Knowledge	Reflection connects new learning with prior knowledge; the larger the students' fund of knowledge and the wider their experience with new material, the better the quality and quantity of their reflection.
Essential Questions	Review of essential questions as prompts improves quality and quantity of students' reflections.
Inquiry-Based Learning	Students' reflections deepen when they are actively studying their own questions in real-world contexts. Reflection enables them to construct new knowledge and new understandings based on their own experience and learning.
Information Seeking Behaviors	Reflection during the information seeking process serves to reduce students' anxiety or discomfort with the search process, helps to focus the search, and provides opportunities for evaluating information found.
Research Models	All research models either implicitly or explicitly include opportunities for reflection in their steps or cycle.
Formative and Summative Assessment	Formative and summative assessments give students opportunities to reflect on their work, research process, information seeking behaviors, and new knowledge. Formative assessment provides students with opportunities to revise their work after reflecting on their progress. Summative reflection prepares students to use their new knowledge and skills in other settings.

Table 8.2 Reflection addressed within *Standards for the 21st-Century Learner*

Standard	Self-Assessment (Reflection) Strategies
1. Inquire, think critically, and gain knowledge.	1.4.1 Monitor own information seeking processes for effectiveness and progress, and adapt as necessary. 1.4.2 Use interaction with and feedback from teachers and peers to guide own inquiry process. 1.4.3 Monitor gathered information, and assess for gaps or weaknesses. 1.4.4 Seek appropriate help when it is needed.
2. Draw conclusions, make informed decisions, apply knowledge to new situations, and create knowledge.	2.4.1 Determine how to act on information (accept, reject, modify). 2.4.2 Reflect on systematic process, and assess for completeness of investigation. 2.4.3 Recognize new knowledge and understanding. 2.4.4 Develop directions for future investigations.
3. Share knowledge and participate ethically and productively as members of our democratic society.	3.4.1 Assess the processes by which learning was achieved in order to revise strategies and learn more effectively in the future. 3.4.2 Assess the quality and effectiveness of the learning product. 3.4.3 Assess own ability to work with others in a group setting by evaluating varied roles, leadership, and demonstrations of respect for other viewpoints.
4. Pursue personal and aesthetic growth.	4.4.1 Identify own areas of interest. 4.4.2 Recognize the limits of own personal knowledge. 4.4.3 Recognize how to focus efforts in personal learning. 4.4.4 Interpret new information based on cultural and social context. 4.4.5 Develop personal criteria for gauging how effectively own ideas are expressed. 4.4.6 Evaluate own ability to select resources that are engaging and appropriate for personal interests and needs.

Source: AASL (2007).

Purpose of Reflection

The use of reflection is predicated on two assumptions:

• Students learn better when they articulate connections to prior learning and real-world experiences.

• Students increase understanding when they contemplate both what (content) and how (process) they learned and how this new knowledge can be used in the future.

Table 8.3 Variables Affecting Student Reflection

Learner Characteristics	• Skill and experience • Knowledge of content area • Motivation • Mental preparation • Sense of safety and security
Environmental Characteristics	• Nature of interpersonal environment • Nature of physical environment
Reflection Task Characteristics	• Stimulus questions, directions, and probes • Format • Quality of feedback • Consequences

Source: Gustafson & Bennett (2002).

Brain-based principles for learning (Caine & Caine, 1990) support these assumptions. Reflection is an opportunity for students to make meaning out of the content they have just learned. The search for meaning is an innate survival mechanism. Living organisms must assimilate, accommodate, and adapt to changes in their environment in order to survive. *Reflection helps students manage and understand their emotional responses to new learning.* Emotions, stress, dispositions, and self-esteem mediate learning and memory. People generally have better recall of information that is emotionally laden or personally meaningful, but have difficulty learning when under stress. Learning involves both the conscious and unconscious. Much learning occurs peripherally, outside of awareness. Reflection is an active, deliberate process that facilitates learning by making the unconscious conscious. The search for broader implications and meanings helps students take charge of their learning, internalize it in ways that are individually meaningful, and connect it to other areas of knowledge (Caine & Caine, 1990).

Environments that nurture academic success provide children with opportunities to reflect on the results of their efforts and to modify them (Diamond, 1999). Ramdass and Zimmerman (2008) report that students' mathematics performance improves when given frequent opportunities to contemplate what they have learned and the nature of their errors after completing a math task. Unrealistically low self-efficacy beliefs, not lack of ability, may lead to math avoidance. Similarly, students who know their own cognitive profile and reflect on their own reading ability demonstrate greater reading achievement than students who know their profile but do not use reflection (Allen & Hancock, 2008).

Influences on Reflection

Characteristics of the learner, environment, and reflection tasks influence quality and quantity of reflective thought (Gustafson & Bennett, 2002) (see Table 8.3). Although reflective ability may be to some degree innate, training and experience contribute to the development of reflective skill (Gustafson & Bennett, 2002). For many students, their experiences in traditional classrooms necessitate training. Reflective learning differs from traditional modes in which students are accustomed to providing facts or recalled information on tests or in essays. In traditional classrooms, students are passive receivers of information. Reflection requires active manipulation of information as demonstrated through higher-order thinking skills (Dyment & O'Connell, 2010). Learning experiences that promote reflection include describing or defining desired behaviors; modeling during classroom discussions; and providing examples for analysis, opportunities for practice, and constructive feedback. Dyment and O'Connell advise directly teaching a system of critical thinking, such as Bloom's Taxonomy, so that students understand the goal and have an appropriate vocabulary. Offering instruction on Kolb's learning styles enables students to evaluate their own styles in relation to the learned content (Dyment & O'Connell, 2010).

Students' knowledge of content area impacts the quality and quantity of their reflection (Gustafson & Bennett, 2002). The ability to reflect on a topic is related to familiarity with that topic. If the students' prior learning has not been accessed, students have less to which they can relate new information and, consequently, less information available for reflective thought.

The strength and nature of students' motivation influence their engagement in reflection. Ideally, students are internally motivated. Reflection offers an opportunity to solidify their learning and consider their accomplishments. It builds self-confidence for successfully completing the assignment, managing their information needs, and solving complex problems (Preddy & Moore, 2005). Classroom teachers and school librarians build students' internal motivation by pointing out the value of reflection and giving feedback during and after reflection. Inquiry-based learning strengthens motivation by involving students in answering their real-world questions. Some students, however, require external motivation in the form of grades or rewards. Unfortunately, external motivators increase the risk of superficial reflection: students write what they think teachers want just to get the grade. To avoid this problem, Preddy and Moore suggest giving points for criteria other than the content of reflection. These criteria include following instructions, using complete and detailed sentences, demonstrating honesty and relevance, and using school-appropriate language.

Closely related to motivation is students' mental preparation for reflection. Students must clearly understand the purpose and expectations (Dyment & O'Connell, 2010). Classroom teachers and school librarians encourage student involvement when they explain the goals of reflection: describe the unit of study, enhance understanding, develop critical thinking skills, and solve a problem. Students need to understand how reflection fits into the unit, how it relates to learning objectives, and how it promotes future learning.

Mental preparation is useless, however, if students do not feel safe sharing their thoughts. Knowing the intended audience impacts the level of reflection and self-disclosure (Dyment & O'Connell, 2010). Students must feel they can communicate honestly without fear of negative consequences or reprisals from classmates or educators. If students share reflections with only classroom teachers or school librarians, they must know their thoughts are confidential. Preddy and Moore (2005) suggest classroom discussions about the importance of privacy and trust.

Creating a safe and secure classroom environment is essential for reflection to occur. Social interaction may promote greater reflection (Gustafson & Bennett, 2002) but only if students trust their classroom teacher, school librarians, and classmates. Classroom teachers and school librarians develop a safe environment by establishing parameters for classroom behavior; demonstrating respect and support for all students; engaging in honest, appropriate self-disclosure; and acting with integrity. Student interaction and class discussions may enhance motivation, prolong engagement, and encourage deeper thinking. In order for this type of exchange to occur, students must know they will not be ridiculed or teased.

Characteristics of the reflection task, such as the nature of the questions, directions, or probes used to stimulate thought, influence the amount and quality of reflection. Reflection is an opportunity to explore the unit's essential questions, to think about the big picture, and to consider possibilities. Probes with evaluative quality will stimulate higher-order thinking skills (Gustafson & Bennett, 2002). Clark (2008) suggests the following probes:

- "What if . . . ?" questions.

- Consider possible consequences for what you have learned: "So, what does this mean? Why does it matter?"

- Compare and contrast.

- Evaluate what you have learned from a variety of perspectives or within different contexts.

- How does this relate to the theory, framework, or rationale?

Fact questions or questions that rely on memory or recall do not work. Probes should stretch students' thinking, make them struggle with ideas, and suggest even more questions.

Formats for Reflection

The format used for reporting or recording reflection shapes quantity and quality. Although many classroom teachers and school librarians rely on journaling (Dyment & O'Connell, 2010; Milam, 2005; Preddy & Moore, 2005), creative alternatives exist. Based on needs assessment, school librarians and classroom teachers choose options for particular class cultures. Reflection can occur individually or in groups. Milam suggests using both individual and group reflection formatively during the information search process. Individual formats include the following:

- Journaling

- Reflective papers

- Oral presentations

- Individual conferencing

- Portfolios

- Posters

- Multimedia productions

- Blogs

- Webpages

- Creative writing

- Questionnaires

Group formats include the following:

- Surveys

- Oral responses

- Pair-sharing

- Peer coaching/mentoring

- Peer observation and feedback

- Small group discussions

- Large group discussions

- Posting to chat rooms, discussion boards, or listservs.

Below is a closer look at three individual and two group formats.

Reflective Papers

Most students do not like to write papers for a multitude of reasons: poor spelling, bad grammar, the length of time that it takes, fear of failure, or feelings of inadequacy. Therefore, for reflective feedback to benefit all, school librarians and classroom teachers offer guided questions or probes such as "If you could complete this unit again, what would you do differently?" and a scaled rubric from most to least acceptable. Usually the rubric accompanies the guided questions or probes; however, it can itself serve as a reflective tool if it has breadth and depth.

Portfolios

Student portfolios allow students to review earlier work; have a place for comments, reflection, and observation; and evaluate their knowledge and skills progress. Students self-assess their dispositions: flexibility, confidence, diligence, creativity, optimism, and assertiveness (Harmin, 1994). Portfolios can be either print or electronic; they provide students a method for archiving materials, documents, and critiques of past and present work.

Students make comparisons, self-evaluate, and set higher inquiry goals. Successful portfolios require structured guidance, instruction, and specific criteria.

Individual Conferencing

Although designed to feel casual and informal, individual conferencing requires careful planning and preparation. Essential questions determine quality of collaborative units; individual conferencing questions determine quality of reflection. School librarians and classroom teachers unfairly influence students' responses when their questions contain bias, nebulousness, or ambiguity. As school librarians and classroom teachers have the conversations, they filter what students think their attitudes should be and what their answers reveal as actual feelings. They predicate their filtering on student familiarity gained through needs and formative assessments.

Surveys

Individual formats are not always efficient; surveys are an expeditious means of reflection. With the number of free online survey makers today, it is possible to entice students' feedback via 10 to 12 survey questions that would indicate reflection on content and information seeking behaviors, both intellectual and emotional. Like any technology tool, surveys, if used too often, become unimportant; and students cease to respect the purpose of the exercise.

Oral Responses in a Group Setting

Inquiry-based process requires essential questions. Oral responses require reflective questions: What part of the research process was most helpful, and why? Aware that students receive body signals and mimic each other in group settings, school librarians and classroom teachers set parameters to enable personal disclosure. All students must know their individual reflections are respected and worthy of consideration.

Whether in individual or group format, the quality of feedback plays an influential role in determining reflective behavior. Providing no feedback substantially reduces quantity and quality of reflective thought (Gustafson & Bennett, 2002). When educators fail to give feedback, students assume that reflective thought is unimportant or unnecessary. Feedback must be fair, equitable, and respectful (Dyment & O'Connell, 2010); otherwise, it will decrease motivation and undermine trust essential for honest and thoughtful reflection. Responding to students' thoughts, feelings, and observations with comments, questions, and probes encourages further elaboration by the student. Ideally, classroom teachers, school librarians, and students engage in reflective dialog with extended and deepened ideas and learning.

Collaborative Reflection

Classroom teachers and school librarians engage in reflection together and individually. Throughout the unit of study, they informally reflect on teaching strategies, classroom activities, and students' responses and information seeking behaviors. They consider what methods work best for which students under what circumstances and why. They adjust their teaching behavior day by day. Does the unit of study address content, information literacy, and technology standards? At the end of the unit, they engage in more formal reflection, ideally in a conversation that addresses the nature of their collaborative effort: What worked? What did not work? What should be done differently in the future? How did the collaboration enhance student achievement?

How did the collaboration contribute to professional growth? Should their roles have been different? Did they allow enough time to plan, prepare, and process? What is the quality of the working relationship? Were there areas of disagreement that could have been resolved with consensus rather than capitulation on one person's part? This last question has the potential to create discomfort; educators, using lack of time as an excuse, are likely to avoid the question. A brief questionnaire using yes/no responses or Likert scales allow classroom teachers and school librarians to evaluate their own and each other's contributions and to provide feedback.

There is strength in reflection as a collaborative tool. Reflection is a look at the total package. Classroom teachers and school librarians have much to learn from and share with each other. Collaboration not only enriches students' learning, but challenges educators constantly to improve their own skills and pedagogy (see Table 8.4).

Table 8.4 A Unit Collaboration Evaluation by School Librarian and Classroom Teacher. For each item, rate how helpful it was in moving the students toward the desired outcome.

Item	Very Helpful	Helpful	Somewhat Helpful	Needs Revision
Posting standards in classroom				
Distributing rubrics to students				
Description of the assignment				
Proposal				
Sample Authentic Intellectual Work				
Graphic Organizers: a. Information Collection Worksheet b. Story Board (rough draft) c. Story Board (final draft) d. Credits (or citations)				
Big6 Model				
Classroom lessons on Solar System				
MLA citation style lesson				
Technology lesson				
Pre- and post- test				

Question	Yes	No	Comment
Did the unit enable students to meet content standards?			
Did the unit enable students to meet the AASL and NETS-S Information Literacy Standards?			
Was the number of days allotted for the unit appropriate?			
Was the division of time between the classroom and the computer lab/media center appropriate?			
Was enough time allotted for each lesson and activity?			
Was the division of responsibilities between the teacher and school librarian appropriate and fair?			
Would you participate in this collaboration again?			

Chapter 9

Technology and Technology's Tools: Web 2.0

The 21st-Century Educational Environment

Daily, educators address workforce preparedness. They resolve to include technology in preparedness because technology influences skills, dispositions, self-assessment, and cognition. It is not difficult to see relationships of technology competencies to workplace tasks. Pedagogically, classroom teachers and school librarians strive to make the digital world an instructional experience for students. It is not enough to have labs full of computers, each classroom with 5–6 computers, and portable computer workstations that move from classroom to classroom on demand. No longer does it suffice for building administrators to brag about the wealth of computer workstations available. Classroom teachers need comfortable experiences with the hardware and released time for receiving software training. They transfer their knowledge to subject area learning that invokes strong positive student responses.

Students want to see value of subject materials to their lives, and incorporation of technology into teaching/learning schema gives them a vision of their lives within the 21st-century world. What the digital phenomenon has created are opportunities to explore new ways to learn and to synthesize, convert, and create. The pedagogical approach parallels "real life." Real life means simply what occurs in daily living and, specifically, what occurs in the workplace. There will be those students who expand their K–12 education with higher learning and others who will move from the classroom into the world of work. For both, it is essential they spend time in school with more than review software, digital games, drill exercises, and information surfing. The world they enter is part of a competitive global age. Partnership for 21st Century Skills (2010) envisions an educational model that blends traditional learning—the 3 Rs (mastery of core content)—with the 4 Cs:

- Critical thinking

- Collaboration

- Communication

- Creativity

Today's students accept the importance of the 3 Rs; but increased traditional rigor without critical thinking, collaboration, communication, and creativity does not improve outcomes. This book has covered inclusion of the 4 Cs in multiple, interwoven, defined ways, such as constructivist learning, inquiry-based lessons paralleled with Bloom's Taxonomy, multiple intelligence strategies, and sensitivity to learning styles. Nonetheless, cognitive development and successful implementation of any skill begin with students' needs assessments.

Because students' daily lives include cell phones, smart phones, Nintendo Wii, Microsoft Xbox 360, iPods/MP3, laptops, tablets, and e-readers, students do not question the presence of hardware; but they do question public-school denial of that hardware's validity. Widespread children's and teens' fascination with electronic devices makes obvious the futility of school-wide banishment. Research is meeting the demand for new and better hardware with no end in sight. Technology is a fertile field for continuing R&D (research and development). Consumers are benefactors, and children and teens are huge consumers.

> "These days, the 'soccer mom' has long been replaced by the 'techno mom' who buys a Leapfrog electronic toy for her baby; lap-surfs with her toddler; has a Wii, Xbox and PlayStation for the kids; puts the spare TV in the child's bedroom; sets her child down for hours at a time to use addictive social media like Webkinz and Club Penguin; and buys a laptop for her preteen so she won't have to share her own computer. In many homes, the computer is now primarily an entertainment device, for downloading music, watching videos, playing games and social networking . . . Parents' behavior and attitudes toward technology are a critical factor in predicting a child's experience with various media" (Hobbs, 2010).

School leaders, main among whom should be school librarians, must bring the forces together. Results of ISTE's (International Society for Technology in Education) student surveys indicate that students feel inadequately taught through technology learning opportunities. Teachers specify insufficient technology knowledge and too little time for gaining knowledge and skill. Collaboration resolves, to some extent, insufficiency and time conflicts by giving two educators more chances for blending favorite hardware tools and software usage into the educational/instructional framework. Harada and Yoshina (2005) suggest there are four themes concerning educational (instructional) technology in curricula:

- Technology as a tool for learning

- Technology as a tool for communication

- Technology as a tool for research

- Social and ethical issues related to uses of technology

Web Evaluation

Successful usage in the library media center (LMC) combines technology for learning and technology as a research tool. To have informed research results, students evaluate websites for authenticity, accuracy, currency, relevance, and authority. If the site is a hoax, there is no *authenticity*. Spotting a hoax necessitates careful scrutiny rather than automatic acceptance. If students settle for one hit on a particular subject, they cannot be assured what they have found is accurate. Comparing information and data guarantees students a greater degree of *accuracy*. How is *currency* measured? Do students check the bottom of an electronic page to validate the date posted? Have there been updates? *Relevance* is meaningless unless students understand the value of their "finds" in relation to essential questions. Last, by going to the home page or About Us page, students determine who wrote and/or posted what they are hopeful of using; there are credentials to verify *authority*.

Additionally, technology as a tool for research incorporates search engines versus web directories; familiarity with online books and journals; availing oneself of subscription databases; use of multimodal formats; understanding citations and bibliographies; and reflection on substantiation of technology as an educational, curricular augmentation. School librarians keep records of student usage; charts visualize their work with web authoring tools, electronic resources, and online databases. School librarians' documentation garners administrative and teacher support. With that support, collaborative units of study with technology components more efficiently prepare students for the real world. Not only do students have exercises within units of study that require technology, but also their use of technology summatively as an authentic assessment tool allows students to delve into Web 2.0 areas with which they are both familiar and unfamiliar. Classroom teachers and school librarians run a risk when they allow students to create with software they have been using in their social networking. Classroom teachers and school librarians reduce the risk when they evaluate Web 2.0 software on a regular basis (see Table 9.1).

Web Evaluation and Social Networking

Allowing students to peruse social networks for gathering and sharing information, for example blogs, IM, e-mail, Twitter, wikis, Facebook, and YouTube, requires judgment calls by classroom teachers and school librarians. Weighing student daily exposure to these sites

Table 9.1 Web 2.0 Evaluation for Reducing Risk and Supporting Collaboration Goals

Criteria	Questions	Considerations	Potential Web 2.0 Tools
Multiple Intelligences and Learning Styles	1. Does the application meet the needs of learners with diverse intelligences? 2. Does it engage students with different learning styles? 3. Is the application multimodal in nature?	Gardner's Multiple Intelligences: • Linguistic/Verbal • Logical/Mathematical • Musical/Rhythmic • Spatial • Bodily/Kinesthetic • Interpersonal • Intrapersonal • Naturalistic Learning styles: • Visual • Aural • Reading/Writing • Kinesthetic • Convergent • Divergent	• Video and podcasts • Photo Story 3 • Animoto • Ed.Voicethread.com • Google Earth • Google Maps • Social networks • Online gaming • Streaming • Smilebox • PicArtia • Flickr • bighugelabs • Webquest.org
Higher-Order Thinking Skills	1. Does the application require the use of higher order thinking skills? 2. How does it engage higher order thinking skills?	Bloom's Revised Taxonomy (Anderson & Krathwohl, 2001, pp. 67–68): • *Apply:* Executing, implementing, using • *Analyze:* Differentiating, organizing, attributing, discriminating, outlining, integrating, diagramming, deconstructing • *Evaluate:* Testing, critiquing, judging, appraising • *Create:* Producing, designing, constructing, synthesizing	• Photo Story 3 • Windows Movie Maker • Ed.VoiceThread.com • Animoto • Edublogs • ThinkQuest.org

Table 9.1 (Continued)

Standards	1. Does the application meet AASL and/or ISTE standards? 2. Can the application be used to meet state standards?	Specify: • Which standard is met • How each standard is met	• Online gaming • Photo Story 3 • Animoto • Create A Graph • Google Earth • Google Maps

against measures like validity and legitimacy will not deter students' personal contact but can help them see critiquing as a formidable means for deciding whether the social network has sound, ethical, personal and academic application. Anyone can post text and visuals. It comes down to layman versus expert. "Expertise" connotes more than hours in front of computer monitors. Expertise contrasts casual knowledge, ordinary use, amateur application, and novice operation. Within workplace preparedness, classroom teachers and school librarians, mindful of the evaluation chart for Web 2.0, create technological situations that heighten students' technological awareness and knowledge. Digital technology makes users not only smarter, but also wiser: (1) wisdom *from* the use of digital technology to grow beyond innate capacity to higher cognitive levels, and (2) wisdom *in* prudent use of technology (Prensky, 2009).

Outcomes are less problematic and bear fruit when students critically tackle Web 2.0 software as an authentic assessment of their understanding, knowledge, and insight. Creativity with Web 2.0 reflects the highest level of Bloom's Taxonomy. Formats for authentic assessment differ for variety of purposes. Just as students extract information for learning in many different ways so, too, they re-form and produce in multitudinous ways metacognitively. Metacognition means knowing when and how to use particular strategies for learning and problem solving. Because of the plethora of Web 2.0 programs, students experiment with ones that meet their individual needs. No longer must students write the ubiquitous report; they have creative license to seek assessment tools that most authentically express their unit learning and new knowledge. Student capabilities move beyond audio and visual representations of their personal likes and dislikes to new levels of expression, demonstrations of their interaction and metacognition with technological processes and resources.

Technology and Essential Workplace Skills

SCANS (Secretary's Commission on Achieving Necessary Skills) Report (U.S. Department of Labor, 1999) describes six essential workplace skills: decision making, creative thinking, ability to conceptualize and imagine, knowing how to learn, reasoning, and problem solving. Inquiry-based units, led by collaborative teams of classroom teachers and school librarians, allow student decision making because students will share their learning creatively, based on their judgments and choices. Strong, planned use of multiple technologies help students conceptualize and imagine. Some students respond sooner than others because of their diverse learning styles, but with essential questions to guide them, all students can reason and problem solve. Having models and processes teaches them how to learn. Due to collaborative flexibility, classroom teachers and school librarians incorporate more techniques that give students constructivist practice with technology. These episodes prepare students to operate fluently in the digital world.

Although the SCANS Report's (U.S. Department of Labor, 1999) overarching competencies cover more than mentioned here, the significance of this list shows how closely correlated the list is to collaboration goals of classroom teachers and school librarians:

- Organizes and maintains information

- Interprets and communicates information

- Uses computers to process information

- Participates as a member of a team

- Understands systems

- Monitors and corrects performance

- Improves and designs systems

- Selects technology

- Applies technology to task

- Maintains and troubleshoots technology

These SCANS competencies align with AASL *Standards for the 21st-Century Learner* and ISTE NETS (National Educational Technology Standards) (see Table 9.2). Students acquire and evaluate information when guided by an appropriate research model. Organizing and maintaining information correlates with analysis, the re-forming of the knowledge into new patterns and means of expression. With interpretation comes demonstration, one communication phase of the inquiry-based learning process. Through it all, students have chances to interact (communicate) and often are placed with partners or small groups. They learn the "two heads are better than one" philosophy that collaboration teaches educators.

Monitoring and correcting performance is the reflection stage. Students review why they chose to do what they did, how well they did it, and what changes they might undertake in the future: improve and design systems. Through it all, technology is a major player from early use of graphic organizers and KWHL charts for establishing prior knowledge to final student projects designed with Web 2.0 software. Selecting and applying technology throughout study units reinforce wise technological decisions. With choices abounding, students are not likely to apply technology to a task without weighing its effectiveness against additional choices. Classroom teachers and school librarians allot fixed time for final projects because of core competency demands. In the end, students maintain their

Table 9.2 SCANS Correlated with Collaboration Goals Using AASL and ISTE NETS Standards

SCANS (U.S. Department of Labor, 1999)	AASL: Excerpted from *Standards for the 21st-Century Learner* by the American Association of School Librarians, a division of the American Library Association, copyright © 2007 American Library Association. Available for download at www.ala.org/aasl/standards. Used with permission.	ISTE NETS: *National Educational Technology Standards for Students*, Second Edition, © 2007, ISTE® (International Society for Technology in Education), www.iste.org. All rights reserved.
• Acquires and Evaluates Information • Uses Computers to Process Information	1.1.4 Find, evaluate and select appropriate sources to answer questions. 1.1.5 Evaluate information found in selected source on the basis of accuracy, validity, and appropriateness for needs, importance, and social and cultural context. 1.1.7 Make sense of information gathered from diverse sources by identifying misconceptions, main and supporting ideas, conflicting information, and point of view or bias. 1.1.8 Demonstrate mastery of technology tools for accessing information and pursuing inquiry. 2.1.4 Use technology and other information tools to analyze and organize information.	3. Students apply digital tools to gather, evaluate, and use information. Students: a. Plan strategies to guide inquiry. b. Locate, organize, analyze, evaluate, synthesize, and ethically use information from a variety of sources and media. c. Evaluate and select information and digital tools based on the appropriateness to specific tasks. d. Process data and report results.
• Interprets and Communicates Information • Participates as a Member of a Team	2.1.5 Collaborate with others to exchange ideas, develop new understandings, make decisions and solve problems 3.1.1 Conclude an inquiry-based research process by sharing new understandings and reflecting on the learning.	2. Students use digital media and environments to communicate and work collaboratively, including at a distance, to support individual learning, and contribute to the learning of others. Students:

(continued)

Table 9.2 (Continued)

SCANS (U.S. Department of Labor, 1999)	AASL: Excerpted from *Standards for the 21st-Century Learner* by the American Association of School Librarians, a division of the American Library Association, copyright © 2007 American Library Association. Available for download at www.ala.org/aasl/standards. Used with permission.	ISTE NETS: *National Educational Technology Standards for Students*, Second Edition, © 2007, ISTE® (International Society for Technology in Education), www.iste.org. All rights reserved.
• Monitors and Corrects Performance	3.1.2 Participate and collaborate as members of a social and intellectual network of learning. 3.1.3 Use writing and speaking skills to communicate new understandings effectively. 3.2.2 Show social responsibility by participating actively with others in learning situations and by contributing questions and ideas during group discussions. 3.2.3 Demonstrate teamwork by working productively with others. Self-assessment strategies: 1.4.1 Monitor own information-seeking processes for effectiveness and progress, and adapt as necessary. 2.4.2 Reflect on systematic process, and assess for completeness of investigation. 3.4.1 Assess the processes by which learning was achieved in order to revise strategies and learn more effectively in the future.	a. Interact, collaborate, and publish with peers, experts, and others using a wide variety of digital environments and media. b. Communicate information and ideas effectively to multiple audiences using a variety of media and formats. c. Develop cultural understanding and global awareness by engaging with learners of other cultures. d. Contribute to project teams to produce original works or solve problems.

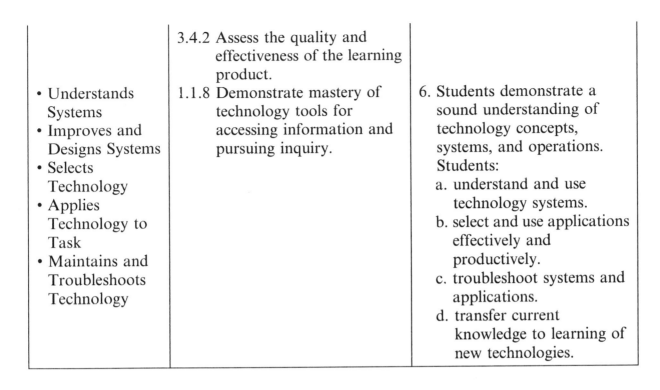

| • Understands Systems
• Improves and Designs Systems
• Selects Technology
• Applies Technology to Task
• Maintains and Troubleshoots Technology | 3.4.2 Assess the quality and effectiveness of the learning product.
1.1.8 Demonstrate mastery of technology tools for accessing information and pursuing inquiry. | 6. Students demonstrate a sound understanding of technology concepts, systems, and operations. Students:
a. understand and use technology systems.
b. select and use applications effectively and productively.
c. troubleshoot systems and applications.
d. transfer current knowledge to learning of new technologies. |

technological growth and skill by participating in future inquiry-based exercises designed through good classroom teachers' and school librarians' partnerships.

Value of Internet Use

Grade by grade, over and over, in different ways, school librarians address the legitimate concern of Internet software value for material gathering. With tens of millions of websites, students view the Internet as a giant answer source. If the information is there, it must be good. The major web player and students' primary access tool is Google. Because of Google's ubiquitous Internet presence and, therefore, its search engine ranking, students conveniently turn to it. Once there, how much attention do they give to the aforementioned evaluation factors (authenticity, accuracy, authority, currency, and relevance)? What matters to them is what is first. A Northwestern University study (Perez, 2010) made unique discoveries in a poll among first year students at the University of Illinois, Chicago. Although Google was not the only mentioned search engine, students put strong trust in it. From 1,060 participating students, 102 were randomly sampled. Results showed students' trust outweighed relevant clues for materials selection.

Barry Britt (2010) from Sounzabound enthusiastically supports social networks and software. He feels social networking most definitely works for sharing ideas, best practices, and communication, just as Harada and Yoshina (2005) see technology as a tool for communication. Some would contend the argument is not about communication but about whether that communication can be turned into active learning. Naturally, classroom teachers and administration require training with the tools. But too often, administrators are left out of professional development programs. Unless administrators get time and practice at hardware/software workshops, they cannot provide tech-enabled experiences for their teachers and students. Administrators judge hardware and software as viable for teaching without full appreciation of gains and benefits derived from classroom unit design incorporating Web 2.0. Mirroring the sentiment expressed by Chicago principal John Price (Fletcher, 2009), many administrators are skeptical of technology silver bullets. Schools know the lingering consequences of the "technology for technology's sake" syndrome. Working with hardware and software, explicitly Web 2.0, with other administrators gives birth to new school visions not only because of the camaraderie, but also because of specific attention to why software such as Web 2.0 can impact when students learn, how they learn, and why they learn. When administrators model technology use, classroom teachers and school librarians boost their examination and placement of Web 2.0 within their collaborative efforts.

The expectation that school librarians speak the technology language is not unreasonable, and allowing students as classroom trainers is effective to a degree. Students, classroom teachers, and school librarians can learn a software piece together; but having an awareness of a multitude of tools gives school librarians in collaboration with classroom teachers more credibility. Classroom teachers' knowledge of and skill with Web 2.0 tools often are narrow. School librarians are typically the "go-to persons" for resources and means of access. School librarians' working knowledge and cutting-edge familiarity with Web 2.0 garner collaborative support. Since school librarians' roles revolve around information in all its forms, school librarians take the technology lead. Daily they exhibit skill as technology specialists by referring to databases and acceptable websites, by setting up displays in multimodal formats, and by handling production of audio/visual presentations. *When students experience successful academic results, they seek school librarians' help with future situations involving social networking and Web 2.0.*

Modeling Technology Usage

Classroom teachers and school librarians model technology usage when they employ web-based assessment tools as determiners of the following:

- Students' needs

- Students' adequate progress throughout units of study (formative)—for example, polleverywhere.com and proprofs.com

- Students' final authentic assessments (summative)—for example, brainpop.com

For measurement of information literacy skill growth in grades 3, 6, 9, and 12, Tools for Real-time Assessment of Information Literacy Skills (TRAILS) is a self-guided, self-administered knowledge assessment online tool (Kent State University Libraries, 2010). School librarians administer it to determine information literacy competency. Online assessment is optimal because of choice, variety, diversity, levels of difficulty, format, and ease of delivery.

Civic Responsibility: Ethical Use of Information

These paperless efforts offer students experience in civic responsibility. Dictionary.com defines civic responsibility as "responsibility of a citizen" and in education, students are school citizens. *Standards for the 21st-Century Learner in Action* (2009) emphasizes "responsibility" as one of the four strands necessary to impact students' academic and personal learning and encourages collaboration for involving students in numerous experiences where they can develop self-efficacy and self-confidence. As part of a civil society, students' Web 2.0 networking participation involves independent, self-governing actions and attitudes. Each Web 2.0 opportunity carries an ethical obligation. Digital enhancement alone does not negate the need for problem-solving ability, critical thinking, good judgment, or intuition (Prensky, 2009). Because of complications and convolutions of web-based publication, text, or audio/video, the regulations are complex. Educators tend to break copyright as often as students because of misrepresentation of guidelines, lack of clarity, naiveté, or time constraints. If students witness classroom teachers or school librarians ignoring copyright, they will take less care themselves, usually because of disappointment or sense of entitlement. TeachingCopyright.org (2010) offers the following four challenges:

- Reflect on what is known about copyright law.

- See the connection between the history of innovation and history of copyright law.

- Learn about fair use, free speech, and the public domain and how those concepts relate to using materials created by others.

- Experience various stakeholders' interests and master principles of fair use through mock trials.

Whatever lessons take students through major copyright snafus, students, classroom teachers, and school librarians need opportunities to test their understanding of the complex issues. Once students understand intellectual property, another concentration is how to make their viewers, listeners, and readers aware of their new knowledge, grounded both in units' lesson strategies and activities and in what was found via research. Citations and works cited must match. If there is internal documentation, that reference shows up on the Modern Language Association (MLA) Works Cited page. If there is a listing on the Works Cited page, internally, there will be a citation guiding readers to the full bibliographic source.

Presently, to say that schools have technology is like saying neighborhoods have houses. Neighborhoods are replete with varied constructions, and schools are equipped with multiple types of technology. Some districts have placed large quantities of hardware in schools; others have either dated or minimal equipment. Yet they all have some digital technology. Homeowners decide what to do with their houses: neglect them, improve basic features, maintain status quo, and make long-range plans for improvement. School librarians and classroom teachers, through coordinated effort, make technology decisions: let technology overwhelm the teaching/learning process, work to develop a user-friendly approach, maintain the status quo (no thinking out of the box), and make long-range plans for improvement. If classroom teachers are not ready to coordinate, communicate, and/or collaborate, school librarians establish technology goals and continue with techniques and strategies that elicit student involvement.

A "faculty fifteen" at scheduled faculty meetings stimulates digital interest and curiosity because the 15 minutes hit hard a particular technology program or issue. If school librarians illustrate technology points with students' synthesized and creative projects, classroom teachers and administration feel either obligated or inspired personally to try the tool.

School librarians' LMC web pages create opportunities for 24/7 teacher, student, and administrative involvement with some online networking tools such as blogs, wikis, Twitter, Technorati, Livebinders, and delicious. If districts filter useful sites, district technology personnel raise the filter when Web 2.0 sites become instructional exercises. When the school year and "faculty fifteen" begin, school librarians limit numbers of Web offerings at a given time but throughout the school year and as the "faculty fifteen" continues, they add more prospects.

Useful Web 2.0 Software

Although covering all worthwhile Web 2.0 software for deliberation during meetings is not possible, school librarians find the following programs requisite to their overview and demonstration list.

1. Photo Story 3 is a free download from Microsoft that provides students with chances to capture photos and images with sound. Audacity is one of the favorite free programs for capturing sounds. To allow viewers to see the work, students save their products through the Photo Story program.

2. Ed.VoiceThread, a multimedia slide show, holds images, documents, and videos. Students record their voices, sound effects, or music like Photo Story. Some differences are the doodling tool and making comments features. As students present their learned, synthesized material, they can write or draw directly to the prepared slides. Participants make comments by using voice (with microphone or telephone), text, audio file, or video (via webcam).

3. Animoto customizes multimedia work including images stored online (e.g. Facebook, Flickr, Picasa), video clips, text, and soundtracks. Once students load their selections, Animoto arranges the productions for viewing.

4. Glogster can incorporate text, graphics, images, links, audio, and video into "Glogs," online posters. Glogster not only offers means for documenting big projects, but also showcases students' work online.

5. Wordle generates "word clouds" from provided text and lets students present text via a different way of thinking. The clouds give greater prominence to words that

appear more frequently in the source text. Students tweak Wordle with different fonts, layouts, and color schemes. To use Wordle as a summative assessment tool, students accompany their Wordles with oral presentations or additional alternative tools.

6. Prezi, an online tool for creating dynamic digital presentations, has free licenses for education. Requiring no software, Prezi projects are accessible from any computer with Internet access. Unlike other presentation programs, Prezi does not use a linear slide approach.

7. Voki allows students to create personalized speaking avatars to embed in extended project offerings.

8. Smilebox, a photo service, lets students make digital scrapbooks and e-cards. Hallmark uses Smilebox for their free ecards.

9. BigHugeLabs has creative opportunities with trading cards, puzzles, magazine covers, mosaic makers, and calendars. Students, preregistered by classes, can sign in without e-mail addresses. Teachers may view and download students' work in an advertisement-free environment.

10. Skype provides voice and video calls with anyone else on Skype. The conference call capability offers class-to-class exchange, whether local, national, or international.

Although incorporation of technology tools for skill and cognitive development requires patience, planning, perseverance, and process, the ideal that all students leaving school be self-supporting, self-actualizing, lifelong learners inspires classroom teachers and school librarians to "take up the gauntlet." Effective technology implementation for teaching/learning happens under inspirational, supportive leadership. In many cases, undertakings require systemic change: change that partners student technology activities with inquiry-based learning, critical thinking, constructivism, research models, authentic assessments, and reflection. Classroom teachers and school librarians, through collaborative efforts, instigate needed change.

Changing Face of Technology

Classroom teachers and school librarians shake up the status quo when collaborations that combine traditional and innovative strategies employing dynamic technology impact academic achievement. Collaborations that blend educational theory concerning technology with practical application within learning situations make winners of students, classroom teachers, school librarians, and administrators. Because of the constantly changing face of technology, classroom teachers and school librarians confront new challenges regularly. Although there has been an interweaving of Internet and the web, the distinction between the two becomes more apparent with the arrival of apps (applications), simpler services than Internet browsing. Apps are less about searching and more about getting (Anderson & Wolff, 2010).

Present traffic on the Internet via browsers shrinks while apps account for more. These platforms depend on the Internet for transport but not the browser for display. The shift to closed, often proprietary, networks is accelerating (Anderson & Wolff, 2010). Interestingly, while nongenerative systems such as apps (applications) provide ease of use and particular securities, which many school districts and parents request and/or demand, the concept runs counterintuitive to the intellectual freedom espoused by the American Library Association. Jonathan Zittrain, author of *The Future of the Internet—and How to Stop It*, equates apps' neat packaging, ease of use, and reliability with their public attraction. However, he calls them tethered threats because manufacturers can remotely control them. Such technologies contain built-in modification capabilities, and end users (individual owners) often are unmindful of ramifications (Marsan, 2008). Since school librarians advocate less filtering, they are always seeking edification and acquisition of facts about cybersecurity's double-edged sword. Beyond abhorrence of hackers and felonious use of the Internet, there is intervention by regulators, a cybersecurity area not well understood by laymen.

> Zittrain cites three ways that manufacturers can control tethered appliances: preemption, meaning that they can design against particular uses; specific injunction, meaning they can remotely change the product in response to legal action such as a court order; or surveillance, meaning they can use the appliance to provide information about the end user to the manufacturer (Marsan, 2008).

Although the emphasis here is on apps' surveillance capabilities, Internet sites, including many aimed at children, similarly track users' online behaviors.

Zittrain is interested in useful and unobtrusive deployment of technology in education. He contends that software-as-a-service websites like Web 2.0 applications interfere with the Internet's functionality for running open source code. For example, if Google Maps were suspended, many mapping applications built on the service would be affected. Since convenient applications are here to stay, to maintain a balance between nongenerative systems and generative Internet usage, collaborative solutions like wikis and blogs address cybersecurity and privacy problems (Marsan, 2008).

Because the role of school librarians relies on ever-extended understanding and knowledge of technology in society—inclusion by individuals, corporations, industry, and education, there is a continuous need to stay current. That is a tough order on top of other important criteria of school librarians' professional position within school environments but an undeniable requirement for the benefit of students who represent society's future.

Chapter 10

Summation

Partnerships, Planning, Processes, Products

Partnership, planning, process, product—each is an association with collaboration, a particularly valued pedagogical concept in present instructional environments. Collaborations between classroom teachers and school librarians demonstrate what educators hope students practice when learning in classroom and LMC settings. Providing collaborative examples benefits both educators and students because when students learn sharing, networking, and communicating as ways to grow academically, classroom teachers and school librarians are more effective within the teaching/learning venue. Their roles are deepened while their students' learning is increased.

Although planning, a key component of collaboration, has both measurable and immeasurable benefits, classroom teachers and school librarians list time as a major deterrent. Nonetheless, there cannot be collaboration without planning. One finds time even if 10 minutes here and there whether in person or by e-mail. Using one of the numerous online communication programs opens avenues for joint efforts: google.doc and drop.io.

The planning both creates and follows a process for students' success. Processes are major teaching tools of school librarians. One of the most important processes is the information seeking method from acknowledging that one needs information to synthesizing learning into new, creative forms for showing what one has learned. Those creative forms, known as authentic assessments, are the final product of collaborative efforts.

Thus, partnerships, planning, processes, and products guide learners through successful skill and cognitive development and add to their storehouses of knowledge, used, through succeeding units of study, for growth and lifelong learning in its many forms and formats. Most educators contend that the young need to learn certain things in order to ensure cultural and social continuity. Basic skill sets are needed before students move from lower to higher thinking levels. The sheer numbers of resources and vast digital offerings create new needs: knowing what kind of information is required; how to locate, sort, and critique findings; and what method to use for synthesizing and creating for demonstration and communication. This emphasis shift takes learners from knowledgeable to knowledge-able (Wesch, 2009). Those with essential questions within inquiry-based learning want adequate information of both quantity and accuracy. One constructivist student aid in the inquiry-based process is the daily reflection that allows students to internalize their experiences. Classroom teachers and school librarians help students to interpret intent of material, which, when understood, leads to more successful effects. Students become more *able* to convert information to *knowledge*.

Data Collection, Modeling, and Brain-Based Principles

Because school librarians know the value of collaboration for library media centers, classroom teachers, students, and curriculum, they undertake the challenge of keeping data and statistics. Taking time daily for their own reflection should include folder building of who used the LMC's resources, why, how, what number, and to what end. Anecdotal inclusion expounds facts and makes them student- and faculty-personal. Since many are leery of statistical manipulation, having firsthand accounts of student involvement, both successes and shortfalls, gives clearer evidence of collaboration's role within teaching and learning. It is possible to capture that students are information consumers, information critics, information producers, and information converters (from a compilation of words and facts to new learning reflected on high-stakes tests). All school districts and administration want to see test scores rise.

Making students knowledge-able educates them for the unknown, for what might come, and for nimble ways of thinking (Perkins as cited in Newell, 2010). To lead learners toward more experiences in nimble ways of thinking challenges educators to include in their processes 12 brain-based principles (Caine Learning Center, 2010):

- Each brain is uniquely organized.
- All learning engages the physiology.
- The brain/mind is social.
- The search for meaning is innate.

- The search for meaning occurs through patterning.

- Emotions are critical in patterning.

- The brain/mind processes parts and wholes simultaneously.

- Learning involves both focused attention and peripheral perception.

- Learning is developmental.

- Learning always involves conscious and unconscious processes.

- We have at least two ways of organizing memory: an autobiographical system and a set of systems for rote memory.

- Complex learning is enhanced by challenge and inhibited by threat associated with helplessness.

When classroom teachers and school librarians incorporate these principles into their goals, objectives, strategies, and activities, they cover, in their partnerships, students' needs assessment, formative and summative assessment, prior knowledge, essential questions, inquiry-based teaching/learning, higher-order thinking skills, information seeking behaviors, research models, reflection, and technology. The first three principles address learning styles and multiple intelligences—the recognition of individualism within a corporate environment, the public school. Whole-body experiences trigger responses expressed in varied ways that reflect styles and intelligences of students. Even when students act disorganized or distracted, there is a uniquely organized part of them that allows them to seek positive responses, more open attitudes, and stronger personal behaviors. Although tolerance is preached today, the practice is far less than public schools wish. Within collaboration, to offer time for exchange and interaction reaps benefits for students and those conducting the study unit. Tolerance is developed through modeling and creation of situations where all students' opinions are valued and students feel validated.

> The innate desire to discover meaning in what one does requires modeling. Students mimic patterns until the patterns become automatic responses.

As students, classroom teachers, and school librarians seek validity, relevancy, and authenticity, offering examples and samples becomes essential. Using research models, though repetitious to classroom teachers and school librarians, allows necessary patterning that school librarians must repeat for each grade, each subject in each information seeking event. Falsely, many educators (and parents) confuse computer manipulation with skills necessary for critically exploring resources, especially digital ones. Emotions mentioned with patterning are attitudes and dispositions as covered in *Standards for the 21st-Century Learner in Action* (AASL, 2009). Besides concurrent processing of parts and wholes, students simultaneously (while either superficially or wholeheartedly participating in research) judge activities in relation to their life experiences and expectations.

Brain-Based Principles and Developmental Learning

Interestingly, students' ability to dual task supports peripheral perception while concentrating. Focus on patterning or design can include recognition of activities as well as extraneous pieces within the information seeking progression. As with all developmental learning, there are conscious and unconscious behaviors concerning modeling and process. Many times, students cannot articulate subconscious feelings exemplified in their work. Classroom teachers and school librarians minimize these unconscious/subconscious reactions, judgments, and emotions by formatively assessing throughout units of study. Giving students reflection time offers the educators glimpses into unconscious/subconscious emotions.

As stated earlier, educators defend some rote learning as a crux for deeper questioning and query. That later, deeper experience builds upon facts (who, what, where, when) and guides students toward more critical thinking. Critical thinking, starting with what students know, relies on students' autobiographical systems: a way in which they relate their learning to their lives, both past and future. That is not such a bad thing since one of the strands of *Standards for the 21st-Century Learner* (AASL, 2007) is self-assessment. Over and over, students assess whether they will use certain learning, why the learning is important, what they should do with it, and how they fit themselves into the learning process.

If classroom teachers and school librarians believe in the brain/mind principles, they, too, believe in possibilities for themselves for initiating change and innovation. They envision diverse learning settings in which digital tools are advantageously used for teaching/learning. Student disruption is minimized because students move at individualized pacing and interact with print, audio, video, and multimodals as their learning styles necessitate. However, there are software and hardware that can cause disruption if classroom teachers and school librarians do not carefully select well-founded means and methods for instructional usage. *More and more online learning is occurring at all levels of public school.* If mentored satisfactorily, online learning is not a disruption; but such computer-based learning can fulfill academic goals not otherwise possible within certain locales.

Collaboration and Instructional Design

Whether utilizing the latest computer hardware, testing the strength of online learning, or having students turn to the beauty of the written word, how classroom teachers and school librarians design their collaborations to fit students' needs and to accomplish desired outcomes is key. Although state standards and standardized tests guide much of what transpires in and out of classrooms, more attention should be on purpose, goal, and aim of lessons. Knowing what classroom teachers and school librarians expect of students by unit's end will channel what and how they introduce materials. Once the goal is clear, objectives support the goal, and strategies and activities support objectives. The entire process is transparent to classroom teachers and school librarians, and rubrics give clarity to students. When given rubrics early in units of study, students see expectations and, point by point, how to reach the goal and objectives. They understand the importance of formative assessment and challenge themselves to have authentic assessments that satisfactorily demonstrate their learning. Students synthesize and create beginning with their prior knowledge and moving through their research to blend both disparate and similar findings into critical cognition exemplified via appropriate Web 2.0 tools. Throughout instructional design, students encounter both print and digital materials. Technology becomes a learning catalyst, not an end in itself.

If instructional design fulfills its intent, students use new knowledge as building blocks for future academic and personal growth. Over and over, they inquire, think critically, draw conclusions, apply knowledge, create knowledge, share knowledge, participate ethically, and pursue personal and aesthetic growth (AASL, 2009).

> The LMC is the curricular hub for inspiring inquiry, research, and information literacy development.

Classroom teachers and school librarians working together create a teaching/learning synergy, possibly better described as a hybrid synergy. A hybrid synergy embraces teaching, learning, technology, pedagogy, and library media centers' services (O'Connell, 2010). School libraries and school librarians act as centers of learning and innovation. Technology will continue to represent innovation and require changes to the way teaching is handled and learning is expected to happen. School libraries welcome change that positively impacts learning; and even though school librarians do not shy away from change, they do not adopt it without grounding it in valid theory and strong pedagogy.

Ultimately, classroom teachers and school librarians are mentors, facilitators, and guides. They seek means and methods to prepare students for whatever societal, cultural, and personal changes occur in their lives. School librarians connect learners to books, websites, and an array of multimodal offerings for strengthening students' basic understandings and base of prior knowledge. Making the connections does not guarantee students' intellectual growth and strengthening because there are challenges encountered when attempting to locate, use, and interpret information. Students must deal with the interferences they face on their way to satisfactory information acquisition. Interferences might be physical:

- Poor sound
- Small print
- Speed of PowerPoint slides
- Appearances like colors of a web page or book drawings

Interferences might be psychological:

- Outside pressures
- Personal goal setting

Sometimes educators overlook:

- Distractions such as excessive student movement within the classroom or music if that is not a student's strong intelligence

- Mannerisms of those presenting the material or communicating the information;

- Confusion created by dated materials

- Confusion from unclear, vague, or incomplete directions

The simplest of communications can be misunderstood. Because communication is a major learning concern for school librarians, they seek to offer information opportunities, each representing goals for 21st-century learners, for developing disciplined, creative, respectful, and ethical minds.

Chapter 11

Valuable Links and Resources

Library Media Centers, Collaboration, and Student Achievement

Topic	URL	Description
Library Media Programs and Student Achievement	http://www.davidvl.org/ Achieve/Project Achievement National.pdf	*Project Achievement (A National Initiative to Collect and Present Evidence that Links Library Media Programs to Student Achievement, 2003–05)* by David Loertscher.
	http://www.laurabush foundation.org/Lance.pdf	*The Importance of School Libraries* by Keith Curry Lance.
	http://www.lrs.org/ documents/lmcstudies/ proof2005.pdf	*Powering Achievement: The Impact of School Libraries and Librarians on Academic Achievement* by Keith Curry Lance.
Collaboration & and Student Achievement	http://www.districtadmin istration.com/viewarticle .aspx?articleid=1682	The Benefits of Teacher Collaboration.

Information Seeking Behaviors

Topic	URL	Description
Information Seeking Behaviors	http://www.librarysupport staff.com/infoseek.html	Information, articles, and links.
TRAILS: Tools for Real-Time Assessment of Information Literacy Skills	http://www.trails-9.org/	Standards-based assessment of information literacy skills for grades 3, 6, 9, and 12.

Prior Knowledge and Essential Questions

Topic	URL	Description
KWHL	http://www.edhelper.com/teachers/ KWL_and_KWHL_graphic_organizers.htm	Custom KWL and KWHL graphic organizers.
	http://www.teachervision.fen.com/graphic -organizers/printable/6293.html	KWL charts on specific topics.
	http://www.graphic.org/kwhl.html	KWHL chart.
	http://www.ncsu.edu/midlink/ KWL.chart.html	Printer-friendly KWHL chart.
Essential Questions	http://questioning.org/mar05/essential.html	Jamie McKenzie's overview of essential questions.
	http://www.oakcrest.net/news/essential.pdf	Brief guide to essential questions.
	http://www.galileo.org/tips/essential_ questions.html	In-depth discussion on essential questions.

Research Models

Topic	URL	Description
Big6™	http://www.big6.com/	Eisenberg and Berkowitz's comprehensive website about the Big6.
	http://nb.wsd.wednet.edu/big6/big6 _resources.htm	Online resources to support the Big6 compiled by a school librarian.

	http://www.janetsinfo.com/big6info.htm	Big6 skills and stages aligned with AASL *Standards for the 21st-Century Learner*, ISTE *National Educational Technology Standards–Students*, and classroom activities.
	http://big6.wikispaces.com/	Big6 wiki.
	http://www.big6turbotools.com/	Sales site for Big6 software.
	http://www.big6.com/go/wp-content/ 2010/02/LMC_Big6-ICT_Curriculum_LMC_MayJune2010 .pdf	*Information, Communication and Technology (ICT) Skills Curriculum Based on the Big6 Skills Approach to Information Problem Solving* by Mike Eisenberg, Doug Johnson, and Bob Berkowitz.
Super3™	http://www.big6.com/search/super3	Super3 resources at the Big6 website.
	http://academic.wsc.edu/redl/classes/ Tami/super3.html	Basic introduction to Super3.
Simple Four	http://sites.google.com/site/marthaale wine/thesimplefour	Martha Alewine's site for the Simple Four.
	http://icts-sc.pbworks.com/The+Simple+ Four	Information about the Simple Four On the SC K–12 Information Literacy and Technology Guide wiki.
	http://www.horrycountyschools.net/ students/resources/search_strategies ___the_simple_four_/	Search strategies for the Simple Four from the Horry County, South Carolina, school system.
SUCCEED Model for Independent Learning Research Cycle	http://www.daltoninternational.org/ Magazine/Dalton/thesucceedmodel.htm	Brief presentation of a seven-step model using an acronym.
	http://questioning.org/Q6/research.html	Graphic representation of the research cycle.

Summative Assessment

Topic	URL	Description
Rubrics	http://rubistar.4teachers.org/	Create rubrics and store them online.
	http://school.discovery education.com/schrockguide/assess.html	Kathy Schrock's Guide for Educators: subject-specific, general, multimedia, and Web 2.0 rubrics.
	http://www.teachervision.fen.com/teaching-methods-and-management/rubrics/4521.html http://edweb.sdsu.edu/triton/july/rubrics/rubric_guidelines.html	Teacher Vision's five-part series on creating rubrics; student-generated rubrics. Guidelines for developing rubrics.
Enhancements and Authentic Assessments	http://www.brainpop.com/	Used to introduce a new lesson or topic, to illustrate complex subject matter, and to review before a test.

Reflection

Topic	URL	Description
Guided Reflection	http://www.edutopia.org/creating-culture-student-reflection	*Creating a Culture of Student Reflection: Self-Assessment Yields Positive Results* by Clyde Yoshida.
	http://www.readwritethink.org/classroom-resources/lesson-plans/involving-students-families-ongoing-973.html	Lesson Plan: Involving Students and Families in Ongoing Reflection and Assessment.
	http://www.higp.hawaii.edu/kaams/resource/reflection.htm	Guide to reflective thinking from the Hawaii Institute of Geophysics and Planetology.

Standards

Topic	URL	Description
	http://www.ala.org/ala/mgrps/divs/aasl/ guidelinesandstandards/learningstandards/ AASL_LearningStandards.pdf	AASL *Standards for the 21st-Century Learner.*
	http://www.iste.org/Content/NavigationMenu/ NETS/ForStudents/2007Standards/NETS_for _Students_2007.htm	ISTE *National Educational Technology Standards–Students.*
	http://www.iste.org/Content/NavigationMenu/ NETS/ForTeachers/2008Standards/NETS_for _Teachers_2008.htm	ISTE *National Educational Technology Standards–Teachers.*
	http://www.p21.org/index.php?option=com _content&task=view&id=254&Itemid=120	Partnership for 21st Century Skills, Framework for 21st Century Learning.

Web 2.0

Topic	URL	Description
Art/Drawing	http://gliffy.com	Flowcharts, diagrams, floor plans, technical drawings.
	http://goanimate.com	Make your own animated characters, direct your own cartoons and watch others' creations.
	http://www.wordle.net	Make "word clouds" from text and give prominence to words that appear more frequently in the text.
	http://www.tuxpaint.org/	Open-source free drawing program for children ages 3 to 12.
	http://blabberize.com	Insert a picture of choice to create a talking image. The trick is making the mouth movement work smoothly and naturally.
	http://school.discovery education.com/clipart	There is a fee for these 3,000 images that are helpful for student projects and other LMC demonstrations.

(continued)

(Continued)

Topic	URL	Description
Audio/Sound/ Music Tools	http://www.pikistrips.com/	Create a photo strip (like a comic strip using photos).
	http://picnik.com	Powerful photo-editing tool—creative effects that can grab photos from Picasa, Flickr, or Facebook, for example.
	http://bighugelabs.com	Considered a Flickr toy, bighugelabs covers jigsaw puzzles, trading cards, posters, magazine covers.
	http://audacity.sourceforge.net	A tool for creating audio files and for recording and editing sounds and podcasts.
	http://www.apple.com/ilife/ garageband	Learn to play an instrument, write music, or record a song.
	http://findsounds.com/types.html	Search the web for sound effects.
	http://thounds.com	Record original music by using a microphone or plugging your instrument into a computer.
	http://www.noteflight.com	Create, view, hear original music in web browser and embed in a personal web page.
	http://www.soundzabound.com/	A royalty-free music library meeting the licensing and technology requirements needed for education. It offers a wide variety of music, audio themes and sound effects for grades K–12.
	http://voki.com	Voki as a free service focuses on creation of avatars for use in blogs and other communication tools.
Books		*Lesson Plans for Developing Digital Literacies* (November 2010) NCTE.

Hardware beyond the PC or laptop	http://www.edutopia.org/cellphonesinclass	This blog post suggests that a pencil is just like a word processor and that a cell phone is a powerful personal computer. Rather than confiscating cell phones as nuisances, the post advises leveraging them as classroom tools. The cell phone may be used as a computation device, a camera, a text-messaging device, a portable storage device, a music player, a word processor, and probably more.
	http://www.ehow.com/how_5257011_use-flip-cameras-classroom.html#ixzz0zbcgHvxb	Flip cameras are ideal for students to use in the classroom because they are small, versatile, and durable. They require no extra cords or software and can be used anywhere by students in grades 2 and up.
Internet storage and collaborative sites	http://www.dropbox.com	Organizational tool for teachers and students accessible anywhere.
	http://sync.in	When multiple people edit the same document simultaneously, any changes are instantly reflected on everyone's screen. The result is a new and productive way to collaborate with text documents, useful for meeting notes, brainstorming, project planning, training, and more.
	http://www.blogspot.com	Create a blog using a variety of fonts and colors; post text, photos, and videos.
	http://technorati.com	A directory of blogs.
	http://wikispaces.com	An easy editor like a word processor for formatting text, inserting images and files, adding widgets, and linking to other pages.

(continued)

(Continued)

Topic	URL	Description
Lists of Sites and Guidelines	http://www.teachersfirst.com/content/edge.cfm	TeachersFirst and Web 2.0 in the classroom.
Media Literacy	http://www.tweentribune.com	Age-appropriate news stories that will interest tweens (generally defined as ages 8 to 14). For web safety, their comments are moderated before publishing.
	http://www.frankwbaker.com/	Media Literacy Clearinghouse: Resources for K–12.
Multimodal Online Tools	http://www.xtranormal.com/	Xtranormal's approach to moviemaking builds on typing. Type something and Xtranormal turns it into a movie on the web and on the desktop.
	http://edu.glogster.com/	With Glogster, students can make interactive posters.
	http://www.smilebox.com/	Add photos, videos, words, and music to create slideshows, greeting cards, scrapbooks, and collages.
	http://ed.voicethread.com	This multimedia tool holds images, documents, and video and allows people to leave comments.
Presentation Tools	http://www.prezi.com	Prezi is on a large canvas like a whiteboard rather than linear slides.
	http://www.powerbullet.com/	Powerbullet is a free presentation program using the Flash format.
	http://www.microsoft.com	Photo Story free download for creating student products that contain images and sound.
Teaching/ Learning Aids	http://www.edutopia.org/back-to-school-classroom-resource-guide	*Edutopia* is committed to highlighting what works in education and providing educators with 21st-century strategies, tools, and resources. Free download.

	http://www.shmoop.com/	Lively learning guides by experts and educators for students and teachers.
	http://www.google.com/a/help/intl/en/edu/k12.html	Apps: They work on mobile devices and enable learning both inside and outside the classroom. There is an app for every subject and every level of instruction—from preschool to higher education.
	http://www.youtube.com/watch?v=1M6ZqTQWjeo	QR Codes and uses concerning books.
	http://www.adlit.org/	Resources for teachers and parents regarding students in grades 4–12.
	http://dictionary.reference.com/	Word of the day, flashcards, gateway to thesaurus and encyclopedia.
	http://www.polleverywhere.com/	Ask students questions and after they vote, get tallied results, and generate reports.
	http://www.proprofs.com/	Quiz maker, brain games, and flash cards.
Video	http://www.skype.com	The free version provides Skype-to-Skype calls, video calls, instant messaging, and screen sharing.
	http://animoto.com/	Videos made with your photos and video clips with music added.
Visuals	http://www.tagxedo.com/	Turns words from famous speeches, news articles, slogans and themes and own words into a visually stunning tag cloud where words are individually sized appropriately to highlight the frequencies of occurrence within the body of text.
	http://www.wordles.com	Turn words inside out; try them backwards; transpose them.

(continued)

(Continued)

Topic	URL	Description
Webpage design	http://maps.google.com/	Click on My Maps to mark your favorite places on your map, draw lines and shapes to highlight paths and areas, and add your own text, photos, and videos.
	http://www.weebly.com/	Easily create personal websites and blogs or establish web presence.
	http://www.pageflakes.com/	Create a page personalized with your interests.
	http://www.google.com/ig	Create a page personalized with your interests.

All links were active and accurate at time of publication.

Internet information and websites sometimes change or become inactive.

Glossary of Terms

Apps: An abbreviation for application. Apps are popular software easily accessible from electronic screens (smart phones, Internet, and computers, for example).

Authentic assessment: A type of summative assessment that allows students to demonstrate their understanding and knowledge through active participation rather than through paper-and-pencil tests. As a project-based evaluation, it allows students to transfer their learning from remembering and understanding to synthesis and creativity.

Bloom's Taxonomy: A range of thinking skills from lower to higher order. The taxonomy reflects learners' knowledge, skills, and attitudes.

Brain-based principles: Learning principles that affect students' responses to teaching, lessons, and classroom expectations. Educators who understand brain-based principles accept students' differing learning styles and create a higher probability of students' academic success.

Classroom culture: The composition of the classroom, both the physical arrangement and student makeup that includes ethnicity, gender percentages, community demographics, and socioeconomic levels. The culture of the classroom affects behaviors and dispositions about the material presented, techniques, strategies, and activities used to accomplish lesson objectives.

Cognition: Ways of thinking to acquire knowledge and understanding.

Collaboration: Partnering for a task, objective, or goal. In the educational setting, the collaborations could be among students, students and classroom teacher, classroom teacher and school librarian, and/or school librarian and students.

Constructivism: A theory of learning based on the idea that learners construct new knowledge by reflecting on their experiences and making connections to prior learning. Jean Piaget advocated that there is a strong relationship between learners' ideas and experiences. Intellectual development and skill development can be strengthened through constructivist techniques, strategies, and activities. Authentic assessment is an example of constructivist expression.

Critical Thinking: A higher-order thinking skill on Bloom's taxonomy that involves analysis, synthesis, evaluation, and creativity. Critical thinking determines how learners use presented content to establish connections with prior knowledge and to draw conclusions.

Curriculum: A set of courses established to represent significant variety and diversity of students' academic accomplishment, sufficient for preparation to enter the next level of schooling or world of work.

Differentiation: Instruction and motivation that accepts student diversity and varied learning styles. Differentiated instruction focuses on students' individual learning needs because students come with their own unique backgrounds and skill, learning, and behavior packages.

Equitable access: A term used in today's educational environment to define fair and impartial student access to technology. It could as easily define just and equal means for exposure to and use of multiple print formats.

Essential questions: Ideas that have no "yes" or "no" answers. Essential questions (EQ) move students beyond what, where, and when to what if, why, and how. Because EQ have no easy answers, students must research, weigh results, draw conclusions, and present their findings.

Formative assessment: Teacher-promoted, school librarian–initiated, or student-directed ongoing evaluation. As periodic and frequent, it provides success measurements for skills, cognition, dispositions, and responsibility, which are components of AASL's 21st-century standards. Formative assessment leads to reteaching when necessary and enhances both teaching and learning.

Information seeking behaviors: Those attitudes and dispositions personified during the research process. Behaviors extend from passive acceptance of tasks, to anxiety and undue concern, to willing, eager participation.

Inquiry-based learning: A process that attempts to offer real-world experiences as well as cognitive and skill development. It includes essential questions, research models, information seeking behaviors, assessments, and reflection.

Instructional design: A systematic process working toward a common goal. The common goal is student achievement with content, skill, and performance objectives, assessment instruments, strategies, activities and materials, and evaluations, both formative and summative.

KWHL: A tool for helping students establish context for the inquiry-based process. The KWHL chart includes "What do I know?" "What do I want to know?" "How can I find answers?" and "What have I learned?"

Learning styles: One's preferred way of learning. Some grasp abstracts; some need more concrete experiences; some actively pursue their inquiry; some benefit most from reflection. Learning styles are usually categorized as tactile (kinesthetic), auditory, and visual.

Literacy: Traditionally, literacy meant the ability to read and write. Today there are multiple literacies, such as information, digital, computer, and media. With any literacy, the key element is the ability to handle information in any format, to express ideas, and to make decisions.

Metacognition: One's ability to understand ways of knowing and one's self, particularly in ongoing cognitive endeavors. It is knowing when and how to use particular strategies for learning and problem solving.

Multiple intelligences: Recognition of individual methods for gaining and retaining information, understanding, and knowledge. Classroom teachers capitalize on students' intelligence profiles by offering multiple routes to new understandings and for demonstrating masteries.

Needs assessment: In preparing lessons, executing strategies and techniques, and creating appropriate evaluations, classroom teachers and school librarians look at student populations:

language proficiency, attention spans, personal interests, classroom culture, dispositions, and other personal criteria applicable to the task at hand.

Partnership for 21st Century Skills: A national organization that promotes local, state, and federal response to student preparation for the 21st century. Student outcomes must blend specific skills, content knowledge, expertise, and literacies.

Pedagogy: The process of teaching referring to strategies and styles of instruction as well as knowledge of and comfort with subject materials.

Prior knowledge: "What do I know?" Students' answers to that question help them establish a framework for new academic tasks. Units of study begin with an overview of the new topic and a look at what students bring with them concerning the undertaking for cognition, knowledge, evaluation, and reflection.

Reflection: Ongoing insight and direction that acts as self-evaluation. The students' personal feedback paves the way for construction of new knowledge. These constructivist connections are wider experiences between what is being learned and what was learned, and from prior knowledge through stages of units of study to assessments. Reflection includes what (content) and how (process).

Research models: Information seeking processes and problem-solving strategies for teaching information literacy to students. Research models, such as the Big6, Simple Four, and Organized Investigator, guide students from essential questions through the inquiry-based process to accumulated evidence for synthesis and evaluation included in an authentic assessment of student learning.

Rubrics: Given at the beginning of new units of study, rubrics offer assessment criteria. They indicate the unit's goal and the measurement of students' learning. Rubrics as indicators of proficiency increase objectivity, provide focus, and visually represent progress.

Scaffolding: Support students need when discovering new knowledge. If students are to formulate essential questions and apply an inquiry-based approach for discovering answers and evidence, educators must provide an instructional design that becomes the scaffolding necessary for student actualization.

Standards: Inquiry-based learning includes content, information literacy, and technology standards. Standards are agreed-upon levels of attainment. Classroom teachers and school librarians in collaboration determine the quality expected in an inquiry-based unit of study.

Summative assessment: Prepares students to use their new knowledge and skills in other settings. When students have rubrics to guide them toward the final expectations of units of study, the summative assessment does not come as a surprise but acts as the foundation for further lessons. Summative assessment allows the learning to become prior knowledge for new undertakings.

Synergy: The whole is greater than the sum of its parts. Classroom teachers and school librarians can produce a combined effect that surpasses their separate inputs. These synergistic outcomes offer students enhanced value when completing units of study.

Synthesis: One of the top levels of Bloom's Taxonomy. Students re-form knowledge into new patterns and means of expression.

Web 2.0: Applications used in the teaching/learning environment that afford students opportunities to synthesize, evaluate, analyze, and create. Web 2.0 is interactive, user-centered, and collaborative. Common software programs used in classrooms are social networks, such as blogs and wikis; audio programs, such as podcasts; and video production tools, such as Photo Story, VoiceThread, and Animoto.

References

Alewine, M. (2006). *The simple four: An information problem-solving model.* Retrieved from http://icts-sc.pbworks.com/w/page/10507141/The -Simple-Four

Allen, K. D., & Hancock, T. E. (2008). Reading comprehension improvement with individualized cognitive profiles and metacognition. *Literacy Research and Instruction, 47*(2), 124–139.

American Association of School Librarians. (2007). *Standards for the 21st century learner.* Retrieved from http://www.ala.org/ala/mgrps/divs/aasl/ guidelinesandstandards/learningstandards/standards.cfm

American Association of School Librarians. (2009). *Standards for the 21*st *century learner in Action.* Chicago, IL: American Library Association Publications.

American Association of School Librarians & Association for Educational Communication and Technology. (1998). *Information power: Building partnerships for learning.* Chicago, IL: American Library Association.

Anderson, C., & Wolff, M. (2010, September). The web is dead. Long live the Internet. *Wired.* Retrieved from http://www.wired.com/magazine/ 2010/08/ff_webrip/all/1

Anderson, L. W., & Krathwohl, D. R. (Eds.). (2001). *A taxonomy for learning, teaching, assessing: A revision of Bloom's Taxonomy of educational objectives.* New York: Longman.

Armstrong, T. (2003). *You're smarter than you think: A kid's guide to multiple intelligences.* Minneapolis, MN: Free Spirit Publishing.

Baltimore County Public Schools. (2005). *Information seeking behavior: A critical thinking and information literacy process model with instructional tools.* Retrieved from http://www.bcps.org/offices/lis/models/tips/

Bloom, B. S., Eglehart, M. D., Furst, E. J., Hill, W. H., & Krathwohl, D. R. (1956). *Taxonomy of educational objectives: A classification of educational goals. Book 1: Cognitive domain.* White Plains, NY: Longman.

Boyles, N. S., & Contadino, D. (1997). *The learning differences source book.* Los Angeles, CA: Lowell House.

Bransford, J. D., Brown, A., & Cocking, R. R. (Eds.). (1999). *How people learn: Brain, mind, experience and school.* Retrieved from http://www .nap.edu/catalog.php?record_id=9853#toc

Britt, B. (2010). Soundzabound. Retrieved from http://www.soundzabound.com

Brown, K. (2009, September–October). Questions for the 21st-century learner. *Knowledge Quest, 38*(1), 24–29.

Brualdi, A. (1998). Implementing performance assessment in the classroom. *Practical Assessment, Research, and Evaluation, 6*(2). Retrieved from http://pareonline.net/getvn.asp?v=6&n=2

Burris, S., Kitchel, T., Molina, Q., Vincent, S., & Warner, W. (2008). The language of learning styles. *Techniques, 83*(2). Retrieved from http://www.thefreelibrary.com/The+language+of+learning+styles.-a0186320605

Bush, G. (2009). Toward a culture of inquiry in a world of choices. *Knowledge Quest, 38*(1), 13–23.

Bybee, R. W., & Sund, R. B. (1982). *Piaget for educators* (2nd ed.). Columbus, OH: Charles E. Merrill Publishing Company.

Caine Learning Center. (2010). *How people learn: Grounded in the 12 brain/mind learning principles.* Retrieved from http://www.cainelearning.com/files/Learning.html

Caine, R. N., & Caine, G. (1990). Understanding a brain-based approach to learning and teaching. *Educational Leadership, 48*(2), 66–70.

Callison, D. (n.d.). *Key words, concepts and methods for information age instruction: A guide to teaching information inquiry.* Baltimore, MD: LMS Associates.

Callison, D., & Lamb, A. (2009). *Models.* Retrieved from http://virtualinquiry.com/inquiry/models.htm

Cherry, K. (2010, May 3). *Forgetting: When memory fails.* Retrieved from http://psychology.about.com/od/cognitivepsychology/p/forgetting.htm

Clark, D. R. (2008). *Critical reflection.* Retrieved from http://www.nwlink.com/~donclark/hrd/development/reflection.html

Clark, D. R. (2009). *Bloom's Taxonomy of learning domains: The three types of learning.* Retrieved from Big Dog, Little Dog web page, http://www.nwlink.com/~donclark/hrd/bloom.html

Coffey, H. (n.d.). *Summative assessment.* Retrieved from http://www.learnnc.org

Cushman, K. (1989). *Asking essential questions: Curriculum development.* Retrieved from http://www.essentialschools.org/resources/122

Deutschman, A. (2005, May 1). *Five myths about changing behavior.* Retrieved from http://www.fastcompany.com

Diamond, M. C. (1999). *What are the determinants of children's academic successes and difficulties?* Retrieved from http://www.newhorizons.org/neuro/diamond_determinants.htm

Dweck, C. (2009). Who will the 21st century learner be? *Knowledge Quest, 38*(2), 8–9.

Dyment, J. E., & O'Connell, T. S. (2010). The quality of reflection in student journals: A review of limiting and enabling factors. *Innovative Higher Education, 35*(4), 233–244.

Eisenberg, M. (2001). *Big6™ skills overview.* Retrieved from http://www.big6.com/2001/11/19/a-big6%E2%84%A2-skills-overview/

Eisenberg, M., & Berkowitz, B. (1987). *Introducing the Big6™.* Retrieved from http://www.big6.com/kids/

Eisenberg, M., Johnson, D., & Berkowitz, B. (2010). *Information, communications, and technology (ICT) skills curriculum based on the Big6 skills approach to information problem-solving.* Retrieved from http://www.librarymediaconnection.com/pdf/lmc/reviews_and_articles/featured_articles/Eisenberg_May_June2010.pdf

Elder, L., & Paul, R. (2005). *The Miniature guide to the art of asking essential questions* (3rd ed.). Dillon Beach, CA: Foundation for Critical Thinking.

Elliott, S. N. (1995). *Creating meaningful performance assessments.* Reston, VA: Council for Exceptional Children (ERIC Document Reproduction Service No. ED381985).

Experience Based Learning Systems, Inc. (2007). Kolb Learning Style Inventory figure.

Fidel, R., Davies, R. K., Douglass, M. H., Holder, J. K., Hopkins, C., Kushner, E. J., Miyagishima, B. K., & Toney, C. D. (1999). A visit to the information mall: Web searching behavior of high school students [Electronic version]. *Journal of the American Society for Information Science, 50*(1), 24–37.

Fletcher, G. H. (2009, May). A matter of principals. *T.H.E. Journal*, 22–28.

Gardner, H. (1983). *Frames of mind: The theory of multiple intelligences.* (10th anniversary ed.). New York: Basic Books.

Gardner, H. (1993). *Multiple intelligences: The theory in practice.* New York: Basic Books.

Gardner, H. (2006). *Multiple intelligences: New horizons.* New York: Basic Books.

Garrison, C., & Ehringhaus, M. (n.d.). *Formative and summative assessments in the classroom.* Retrieved from http://www.nmsa.org/portals/0/pdf/publications/Web_Exclusive/Formative _Summative_Assessment.pdf

Gustafson, K. L., & Bennett, W., Jr. (2002). *Promoting learner reflections: Issues and difficulties emerging from a three-year study.* Retrieved from http://www.dtic.mil/cgi-bin/GetTRDoc ?AD=ADA472616&Location=U2&doc=GetTRDoc.pdf

Hadro, J. (2010, May). Meta-study distills reports on information-seeking behavior. *Library Journal.* Retrieved from http://www.libraryjournal.com/

Harada, V. H., & Yoshina, J. M. (2005). *Assessing learning.* Westport, CT: Libraries Unlimited.

Harmin, M. (1994). *Inspiring active learning: A handbook for teachers.* Alexandria, VA: Association for Supervision and Curriculum Development.

Hobbs, R. (2010, July 19). A computer doesn't make kids smart. *Philadelphia Daily News.* Retrieved from http://www.philly.com/

International Society for Technology in Education (ISTE). (2007). *National Educational Technology Standards for Students* (2nd ed.). Retrieved from http://www.iste.org/standards/ nets-for-students.aspx

International Society for Technology in Education (ISTE). (2008). *National Educational Technology Standards for Teachers.* Retrieved from http://www.iste.org/standards/nets-for -teachers.aspx

International Society for Technology in Education (ISTE). (2010). Retrieved from http:// www.iste.org

Kearsley, G. (2010). *Constructivist theory (J. Bruner).* Retrieved from http://tip.psychology.org/ index.html

Kent State University Libraries. (2010). *TRAILS: Tools for real-time assessment of information literacy skills.* Retrieved from http://www.trails-9.org/

Koelsch, N., Estrin, E., & Farr, B. (1995). *Guide to developing equitable performance assessments.* San Francisco, CA: WestEd. (ERIC Document Reproduction Service No. ED397125).

Kolb, D. A., Boyatzis, R. E., & Mainemelis, C. (2000). Experiential learning theory: Previous research and new directions. In R. J. Sternberg & L. F. Zhang (Eds.), *Perspectives in cognitive, learning, and thinking styles.* Hillsdale, NJ: Lawrence Erlbaum.

Kuhlthau, C. (2007). Reflections on the development of the model of the Information Search Process (ISP): Excerpts from the Lazerow Lecture, University of Kentucky. *Bulletin of the American Society for Information Science and Technology, 33*(5), 32–37.

Kuhlthau, C. (2010). *Information Search Process.* Retrieved from http://comminfo.rutgers.edu/ ~kuhlthau/information_search_process.htm

Kuhlthau, C. C., Maniotes, L. K., & Caspari, A. K. (2007). *Guided inquiry: Learning in the 21st century*. Westport, CT: Libraries Unlimited, Inc.

Lance, K. C., Welborn, L., & Hamilton-Pennell, C. (1993). *The impact of school library media centers on academic achievement*. Castle Rock, CO: Hi Willow Research and Publishing.

Loertscher, D., & Woolls, B. (2002). *Information literacy: A review of the research*. Salt Lake City, UT: Hi Willow Research and Publishing.

Loertscher, D. V., Koechlin, C., & Zwaan. S. (2005). *Ban those bird units! 15 models for teaching and learning in information-rich and technology-rich environments*. Salt Lake City, UT: Hi Willow Research and Publishing.

Makela, C. (2003, January 24). *The Virginia Advocate for Library Media Specialists*. Richmond, VA: Virginia Educational Media Association.

Marsan, C. D. (2008, April 9). How the iPhone is killing the " 'Net." *Network World*. Retrieved from http://www.networkworld.com/news/2008/040908-zittrain.html?page=4

Martzoucou, K. (2005). A review of web information seeking research: Considerations of method and foci of interest. *Information Research, 10*(2). Retrieved from http://informationr.net/ir/10-2/paper215.html

Marzano, R. J., Pickering, D., & Pollock, J. E. (2001). *Classroom instruction that works: Research-based strategies for increasing student achievement*. Alexandria, VA: Association for Supervision and Curriculum Development.

McKenzie, J. (2005). Essential questions. *The Question Mark, 1*(5). Retrieved from http://questioning.org/mar05/essential.html

Milam, P. (2005). The power of reflection in the research process. *School Library Media Activities Monthly, 21*(6), 26–29.

Milbury, P. (2005, May–June). Collaboration: Ten important reasons to take it seriously [Electronic version]. *Knowledge Quest, 33*(5).

Newell, T. S. (2009). Examining information problem-solving instruction: Dynamic relationship patterns mediated by distinct instructional methodologies. *School Libraries Worldwide, 15*(2), 49–76.

Newell, P. (Interviewer), & Perkins, D. (interviewee). (2010). *Interviews concerning the future of understanding: Patrick Newell talks to David Perkins*. Retrieved from http://www.21foundation.com

Newmann, F. M., King, M. B., & Carmichael, D. L. (2007). *Authentic instruction and assessment: Common standards for rigor and relevance in teaching academic subjects*. Des Moines, IA: Iowa Department of Education. Retrieved from http://centerforaiw.com

O'Connell, J. (2010). *Hybrid synergy—the future of school libraries*. Retrieved from http://heyjude.wordpress.com/

Palm, T. (2008). Performance, assessment, and authentic assessment: A conceptual analysis of the literature. *Practical Assessment, Research, and Evaluation, 13*(4), 1–11.

Partnership for 21st Century Skills. (2010). Retrieved from http://www.p21.org/

Perez, S. (2010, July 29). *So-called "digital native" not media savvy, new study shows*. Retrieved from http://www.readwriteweb.com/archives/so-called_digital_natives_not_media_savvy_new_study_shows.php

Piaget, J., & Barbel, I. (1969). *The psychology of the child*. New York: Basic Books.

Preddy, L., & Moore, J. (2005). Key words in instruction: Student journals. *School Library Media Activities Monthly, 21*(7), 32–35.

Prensky, M. (2009). H. sapiens digital: From digital immigrants and digital natives to digital wisdom. *Innovate, 5*(3). Retrieved from http://www.innovateonline.info/index.php?view =article&id=705

Ramdass, D., & Zimmerman, B. J. (2008). Effects of self-correction strategy training on middle school students' self-efficacy, self-evaluation, and mathematics division learning. *Journal of Advanced Academics, 20*(1), 18–41.

Reigeluth, C. M., & Garfinkle, R. J. (1994). *Systemic change in education.* Englewood, NJ: Educational Technologies Publications.

Roe, M. (1995). *Working together to improve health—a team handbook.* Queensland, Australia: University of Queensland.

Russell, S. (2001–2002). *Teachers and librarians: Collaborative relationships.* Syracuse, NY: ERIC Digests (ERIC Documents Reproduction Services No. 444605).

School Library Media Services South Carolina Department of Education. (2009). SC *K–12 ICT scope and sequence.* Retrieved from http://scschoollibraries.pbworks.com

South Carolina Department of Education. (2006). *IMPACT: Teaching and learning for the 21st century: Skills guide.* Retrieved from http://icts-sc.pbworks.com

Stafford, T. (2009). Teaching students to form effective questions. *Knowledge Quest, 38*(1), 49–55.

Stiggins, R. (2009). Assessment for learning in upper elementary grades. *Phi Delta Kappan, 90*(6), 419–421.

Sutliff, R. I., & Baldwin, V. (2001). Learning styles: Teaching technology subjects can be more effective [Electronic version]. *Journal of Technology Studies, 27*(1).

Sweet, D. (1993). *Performance assessment.* Retrieved from http://www2.ed.gov/pubs/OR/ ConsumerGuides/perfasse.html

Teaching Copyright. (2010). Retrieved from http://www.teachingcopyright.org

Thomas, N. P. (2004). *Information literacy and information skills instruction.* Westport, CT: Libraries Unlimited, Inc.

Tomlinson, C. A. (2001). *How to differentiate instruction in mixed ability classrooms* (2nd ed.). Alexandria, VA: Association for Supervision and Curriculum Development.

U.S. Department of Labor. (1999). *Skills and tasks for jobs: A SCANS report for America 2000.* Retrieved from http://wdr.doleta.gov/opr/FULLTEXT/1999_35.pdf

V&A Museum of Childhood. (2010). *Figures in education—19th and 20th centuries: John Dewey.* Retrieved from http://www.vam.ac.uk/moc/childrens_lives/education_creativity/ 19_20_centuries/index.html

Walker-Dalhouse, D., Risko, V. J., Esworthy, C., Grasley, E., Kaisler, G., McIlvain, D., & Stephan, M. (2009). Crossing boundaries and initiating conversations about RTI: Understanding and applying differentiated classroom instruction [Electronic version]. *Reading Teacher, 63*(1), 84–87.

Wesch, M. (2009, January 7). *From knowledgeable to knowledge-able: Learning in new media environments.* Retrieved from http://www.academiccommons.org/commons/essay/ knowledgable-knowledge-able

Wiggins, G. (1998). Research news and comment: An exchange of views on "Semantics, psychometrics, and assessment reform: A close look at 'authentic' assessments." *Educational Researcher 27*, 20–21. DOI:103102/0013189X027006019.

Winking, D. (1997). *Critical issue: Ensuring equity with alternative assessments.* Retrieved from http://www.ncrel.org/sdrs/areas/issues/methods/assment/as800.htm

Winking, D., & Bond, L. (1995). *Transforming reading and learning in urban schools through alternative assessment.* Oak Brook, IL: North Central Regional Educational Laboratory.

Wolf, S., Brush, T., & Saye, J. (2003). The big six information skills as a metacognitive scaffold: A case study. *School Library Media Research Online, 6.* Retrieved from http://www.ala.org/ala/mgrps/divs/aasl/aaslpubsandjournals/slmrb/slmrcontents/volume62003/bigsixinformation.cfm

Zimmerman, N. (2002). Pappas and Tepe's pathways to knowledge model. *School Library Media Activities Monthly, 19*(9), 24–27.

Index

About the Authors

VIRGINIA L. WALLACE, a retired professor of the School of Library and Information Science at the University of South Carolina in Columbia, has a doctorate in instructional technology and distance education. Wallace has written *School New Shows: Video Production with a Focus*.

WHITNEY NORWOOD HUSID has a doctorate in clinical psychology and is currently working on a master's degree in library and information science at the School of Library and Information Science at the University of South Carolina.